Winning in One-Designs

Dave Perry

"I first read Dave Perry's authoritative book on one-design racing on my way to a junior championship. Like a student cramming for a test, I devoured his sailing techniques and philosophies. From race preparation to psychology to strategy – starting techniques, understanding windshifts, and downwind positioning – the one-design expert presents the elements of racing in a way that makes you feel that he's writing to improve your game. I still go back to *Winning in One-Designs* to freshen up on tactics and boatspeed concepts or to think about a racing goal."

— Josh Adams, "The Best Books for Sailors"
SAIL

"This book covers every aspect of sailing competition from the importance of earliest preparation to the crossing of the finish line and the winning gun."

— *Sailing Inland & Offshore*

"★ ★ ★ ★! It covers tactics, rules, boat and crew preparation, sail and rig setup... A great book for the intermediate to advanced competitor."

— aigy@efpasia.com
amazon.com

OTHER BOOKS BY DAVE PERRY

Understanding the Racing Rules of Sailing

Dave Perry's 100 Best Racing Rules Quizzes

The material in this book originally appeared
in *Yacht Racing/Cruising* magazine.

TO CONTACT US SAILING

PO Box 1260, 15 Maritime Drive
Portsmouth, RI 02871 USA

Phone: 401 683-0800
Fax: 401 683-0840
Infofax: 888 US SAIL-6

info@ussailing.org
www.ussailing.org

ISBN 0-9762261-4-6

FOURTH EDITION

Cover photograph by Billy Black

Dave Perry

Winning in One-Designs

Introduction by Peter Isler

Illustrations by Brad Dellenbaugh
and Mark Smith

FOURTH EDITION

This book is

dedicated to my grandfather,

Northrop Dawson

ACKNOWLEDGEMENTS

I want to say thank you to my parents who
first taught me how to sail and have been totally
supportive of my interest and obvious addiction
to both racing and teaching. And just as I thank
all my sailing instructors and the friends I've made
through sailing over the years for sharing their
love for the sport with me, I'd like to thank, and
mention here, several friends who have had a
special impact on my teaching: Dave Dellenbaugh,
Brad Dellenbaugh, Peter Isler, and Major Hall.

Contents

PREFACE

I DID MY FIRST RACING SEMINAR for a group of enthusiastic frostbiters at the American Yacht Club in Rye, New York, in the fall of 1977. Since then I've led well over 200, throughout the U.S. and in several countries around the world. The beauty of these short, intensive seminars is that the level of motivation to learn among the participants is extremely high; the only unfortunate aspect is that they end too soon and are repeated too infrequently.

It's been said that in a teaching situation it is the teacher who learns the most. Nothing else I have ever done has improved my own racing more than teaching. Through working at perfecting the seminars, I have learned to put myself in the place of the sailors I am teaching to see more clearly what it is they are experiencing and what things are inhibiting their learning curve. I've also learned not to look at racing in terms of a whole race, but instead to break it down into the many elements that must be thought through and mastered before any of us can set our sights on winning.

Each of the chapters here is written directly from my experiences in both racing and teaching. In the seminars I've tried many different approaches to explaining the material, and the chapters reflect the ones that received the best feedback for being the most clear, understandable, and helpful.

Someone recently asked me what we the most significant thing I had learned over my last five years of actively racing and leading seminars. Without a doubt it's that I've learned how to learn and improve myself. I've seen the tremendous value in not looking outward to measure myself and against other sailors or previous accomplishments but instead looking inward to identify all my own personal strengths and many weaknesses that need help. And as a result I'm experiencing new waves of satisfaction and energy as I improve and close in on mastering areas not only where I was previously weak, but to which, in many cases, I was completely oblivious.

I'm confident that the following chapters identify and thoroughly address most of the major elements in racing sailboats. And to the sailors who can put as much energy and enthusiasm into their learning as they can into their racing, I promise they will find each chapter loaded with useful information.

For a complete analysis of the racing rules, see my book *Understanding the Racing Rules of Sailing*.

Good luck, and enjoy your improvement!

Dave Perry

Learning From Perry

Peter Isler

IT BEGAN as another very ordinary race in the 1979 Soling North Americans. Dave (who was my middle crew) called for a weather-end start and a quick tack toward the right side. I kidded him about his predictability. He loves that opening move, and I had become fairly talented at pulling it off most of the time. At the starting gun we were moving at the committee boat with some 50 odd boats to leeward. We tacked to port and began the long trek to the right corner. Over the course of the tack, Buddy Melges and crew powered through to leeward of us and opened up a three-boatlength lead. That soon became a minor problem, however, as a 35-degree port lift pinwheeled the entire fleet to windward and ahead of us. When we finally bailed out of the right side and began taking transoms, the cards did not look good for a miraculous comeback, but we worked hard, and though we reached the windward mark deep in the 40s, we had Buddy right behind us.

That is the point where the race began to take on an extraordinary quality. Dave unclipped his hiking hobbles and moved aft of me – an unheard-of maneuver for the middle crew during a race. He lifted the cooler (stocked with ice, water, Gatorade and Coke) and placed it on the aft deck. Rubbing his hands together, he looked back and asked, "Okay, Buddy, what'll it be?" Buddy ordered a Scotch and soda, but Dave said he would have to settle for chocolate chip cookies instead, and he began flinging Chips Ahoys at Melges's surprised crew. Then out came Dave's cassette player, and we raced along to the tunes of Charlie Daniels. "Turn it up" came the request from the other boat, and I thought to myself, this is supposed to be our "serious" Olympic effort?

But soon my forward crew, Tucker Edmundson, and I were feeling remarkably good, considering our position in the race. When we reached the jibe mark we were feeling so loose that we pulled one of those classic college racing moves – we didn't jibe. Over 50 boats were headed for the leeward mark in single file, all on a port run. But we continued on starboard for several minutes, then jibed and reached into the mark with a much faster angle. We rounded more than 20 boats ahead of Buddy!

We all know that sailing is supposed to be enjoyable, but it's people like Dave who keep reminding us of this. "We are serious on the race course," explains Brad Dellenbaugh, Dave's forward crew in his current Soling campaign, "but while being serious Dave makes it fun for everyone." Brad recalls a conversation with Australian Ian McDiarmid, who was part of the crew that won the Soling Worlds in March, 1982 when Dave and his crew were a close third. "When I got involved with Mark" [Bethwaite, the skipper], said Ian, "we were very intense about our sailing and treated it like business. But at the Worlds we really enjoyed racing against you guys. You did so well and still had fun, and I started rethinking what this whole thing was about." Whether he is throwing frisbees at the Rumanians during a long postponement or making a friendly comment on the race course, Dave makes a habit of generating good will in the sport.

It was mainly Dave's tactical ability, however, that made him first choice for middle crew in my 1980 Soling Olympic effort. After years of racing against him in Lightnings and Lasers and sailing as his teammate at Yale, I had come to respect Dave's keen tactical ability. Nell Taylor, who crewed for Dave in college in the mid-1970s, remembers his early confidence in crowded situations. "Tight quarters didn't bother him and he was never afraid to try to stick it in at marks." It was probably this daring, let's-see-what-happens style that helped Dave get so good at the rules and boathandling. It also forced him to encounter almost every possible tactical situation, and this, combined with his elephant-like memory for racing situations, gave him a wide base of experience from which to draw. During the years he sailed with me, he taught me to be a much more disciplined tactical sailor.

Many people compare the sport of sailing to the intellectual challenge of chess. Dave is one of the few people I know who has studied the tactics of our game like a science on the course, but also in his imagination. Nell remembers those early morning drives to collegiate regattas: "We had a pact that I wouldn't talk to him because he wanted to go through every possible situation in his mind. We wouldn't practice much, but he would be practicing in his head. Then driving home he would be filing away everything that had happened, and the regatta wasn't over until he had finished thinking about it." Sometimes that took a while and he was often found at mealtime pushing around a bunch of knives and forks to illustrate a point.

Part of Dave's confidence stems from his strong working knowledge of the racing rules. He is a US SAILING certified Senior Judge and a member of the Appeals Committee and is continually pondering new situations with other rules experts. Despite Dave's interest in the rules, however, he has a reputation for being lenient on the course. He always gives people the benefit of the doubt, often letting close situations go by without protest. Brad feels this is part of Dave's desire to make and keep friends in the sport. "He thinks it will all come back, because it's such a closed sport. You will always see sailors again, and if you're nice to them, they'll be nice to you."

For Dave, the rules define how to play the game, and they determine what's fair and not fair. "He likes to push everything to the limit," says Nell, "yet he wants it to be a gentleman's sport. He would get really upset if someone started playing dirty, because they'd be destroying the game." Dave respects sailors like Dave Curtis who sail cleanly and win races by relying on speed and strategy. Before the 1980 Olympic Trials, he, Tucker, and I had long deliberations about how aggressive we should be in the final and most important regatta of our campaign. Dave is continually ruminating about what he calls the ethics of the sport.

It has been interesting to watch Dave's development in the sport through the years, not only as a friend, but as a fellow competitor. There was a time when he made very little effort preparing his boat or worrying about fine tuning boatspeed adjustments. When rotating into a new boat in an intercollegiate round robin series, for example, most skippers would test and adjust literally every control on the boat prior to the Start. But Dave would just jump in, check the condition of the hiking straps, and go. Yet he did just as well. "For him, the outhaul or cunningham made little difference," explains Nell, "it was how you started and sailed."

Over the years, however, Dave has worked hard to develop his knowledge of the finer aspects of sail trim and boat tuning. His involvement in several Olympic campaigns has been partly responsible for this, and his Soling campaign was a well-organized, serious affair leaving almost no stone unturned. Because Dave often takes time to help other sailors and is very free about sharing information (he figures that's the best way for everyone to improve), he has made it easier for himself to pick up information from other sailors. By asking questions of and sailing with sailmakers and other talented boatspeed technicians, Dave has learned a lot.

Of course, Dave is probably as well known for his teaching role as he in for his sailing. His seminars and articles have reached thousands of racers at all levels. He has the rare ability to put a group at ease, perhaps because of his good humor and the fact that he doesn't pretend to be better than anyone else. According to Nell, Dave is a successful teacher because the first thing he usually decides to do is address people's fears and anxieties. She recalls one windy women's clinic where they were all about to go out on the water for the first time. "I know you're all afraid of capsizing," said Dave, "so the first thing we're going to do is have everyone capsize." The adage that claims no one learns more than the teacher is quite true in this case. Dave's role as teacher and writer and all the hours spent analyzing races during his seminars have been invaluable to his racing.

Dave is also very active politically in the sport. He is involved with several US SAILING committees and is a leader in the area of junior sailing. He's a good example of a sailor taking an active interest in the direction of the sport and always trying to make it better for the future.

Whether you are sailing with or against him, Dave makes racing more fun. Though most of us tend to limit our verbal contact on the course to rule-related hails at critical moment, Dave is often making some colorful remark that breaks the tension. And even when things are close, Dave will make an effort to acknowledge the skill of a competitor. In the 1980 Prince of Wales match racing series, for example, Dave sailed against the eventual winner, John Jennings, in the final round. In one start Dave appeared to be in control, tailing Jennings on port tack down the line. As Jennings passed to leeward of the committee boat, he continued for a length and then luffed into the wind. Dave countered by luffing up to windward and abeam. As the time passed, both boats began to lose steerage. Finally Dave realized he'd better bail out or he would soon drift down and foul Jennings. As he started to tack onto starboard, he saw that he could not clear the stern of the committee boat. Jennings had suckered him in and pinned him. In a last-chance effort Dave's crew radically backed the jib to port, and the boat fell off onto port tack, missing Jennings's stern by inches. As he sailed off, a relieved Dave turned to Jennings and smiled saying, "Hey, that's a pretty good move!" "Yeah, it works... sometimes," came Jennings's reply.

Paul Elvström once noted that the people we meet and the friendships we make are the real trophies of our sport. We bring our varied personalities into the game and in return we get friendships and insights into human nature that are true treasures. Dave is one of those special people who can open everyone's eyes a little wider to the rewards of our game.

Profile: Peter Isler

If you had to pick one American sailor to call a "Jack of all trades," it just might be Peter Isler originally from Norwalk, Conn. From high-performance sailboarding to championship dinghy racing to involvement in the world's premier offshore events, Peter has done almost everything and done it well. Competing in a lot of different classes, including both dinghies and big boats, has kept me interested and taught me new things," says Peter, whose escapades include crewing on 1982 SORC winner Retaliation, *winning the 1982 US SAILING team race championship, and being tactician for Dave in their wins of the 1983 and 1984 Congressional Cup. In 1987 and 1988 he won the America's Cup as navigator aboard* Stars and Stripes, *and has been a competitor as well as an expert commentator during several America's Cups since.*

Preparation

CHAPTER 1

Formula for Success

HAVE YOU EVER tried to explain to a non-sailor what makes sailing so fascinating and challenging, or harder yet, justify why it often seems that the only thing sailors ever think and talk about is sailing? When I was working out in the local college gym for the Laser Worlds to be held in Australia, in the course of friendly conversations I was repeatedly asked which sport I was in training for. I answered "sailing" and, with distressing regularity, was met with a somewhat confused "Oh," and then silence.

My first reaction was to rush in with a heartfelt explanation of the mental and physical complexities of the sport, followed by a vigorous demonstration of the many positions the sailor assumes throughout the race. But just as quickly I realized that most of these people had little in their backgrounds with which to relate to what I was talking about. And besides (they probably thought), sailing is never on ABC's Wide World of Sports, except for the time those guys burned their boat in the 1976 Olympics. So how important could it be, anyway?

Finally, after much thought and a few rapid bench presses to work up a sweat, I cornered a particular skeptic and put it to him this way: "Take pro football – a pretty complex sport, right? But every game is played on the same size field, in the same amount of time, against the same number of players, week after week, all over the country. Now imagine, just for a minute, that every field was different in size; that, in fact, the boundaries continually changed during the game. Furthermore, the playing surface moved along under the feet of the players and varied in speed and direction throughout the game. In addition, some areas of the field were soggy, others icy, and still others sandy, with irregular one-foot-high ridges running all over.

"The game would still be the intricate offense vs. defense with the high premium on excellent individual performance. But there would be only 11 guys per team: no specialist teams, no offensive unit separate from the defensive unit, no punt return team, and no guy to come out just to kick the extra point. In fact, there would be no substitutes, no trainers, and no coaches high up in the grandstands looking down on the game, analyzing the upcoming defensive formations and quickly radioing down the correct play or the offense to use." (My mind raged with the image of a sky full of blimps hovering over the entire race course radioing tack after tack to their sailors, while little rubber dinghies shoveled in fresh skippers and crews at strategic points in the race.)

By now, though I was not sure he was quite getting the point, my skeptic was beginning to show distinct signs of intimidation and had definitely begun to rethink his image of sailors. I was having a great time. "In addition," I continued, "there would be no referees passing instant judgments on rule infractions. Rather, the infractions would be noted down and, after the game, those involved would appear before a panel of austere and knowledgeable judges, who may or may not have watched the game. Imagine Mean Joe Green accusing Dick Butkus of holding him. Both gentlemen would have the opportunity to state what happened, question each other to determine the exact place and nature of the alleged infraction, and call witnesses to aid in their case if…"

"But all that could take forever!" my skeptic suddenly blurted out.

And with active restraint to a huge inner grin that went from ear to ear, I answered politely, "Yes, it could." My skeptic had begun to see the light.

WHEN YOU REALLY STOP to think about it, sailing is possibly the most complex sport in the world. I've listed below, in no particular order, some of the many traits the sport requires of its top competitors:

- The five senses must be acute and sensitive to everything going on around them. Some even definitively claim that the top sailors possess a sixth sense, given to them at birth, located in their lower back region;

- Pinpoint accurate judgment and timing to place your boat where you want it, when you want it, and how you want it;

- The difficult ability to make quick decisions (which are also correct) under the constant pressure of ever-changing variables and talented competitors;

- Sufficient intellect to be able to rationally assess all the variables of a situation and apply them offensively and defensively to the race;

- Each individual competitor to deal psychologically with some difficult emotions – disappointment, frustration, anger, greed. We also have to deal with our egos and, perhaps most important, our relationships with others in the boat and in the race. Though no scientific corollary has yet been published, sailors, as people, tend to be frighteningly Jekyll-and-Hyde-like. Some of the nicest guys on land can be the meanest &#!£@!s on the water. Unfortunately, it often goes beyond the race.

- Some, and in many cases, extreme physical conditioning and strength. I wonder how many people actually stretch out or warm up before sailing, though I know too well the stiff back and sore muscles after a seemingly relaxed weekend of racing that I could have avoided with a minimum of warming up.

- The ability to get one's boat into the best possible condition, to achieve equal or superior speed and, almost more important, to prevent breakdowns.

- Finally, it requires that we be our own counselors-at-law, our own trainers, our own pit crews, and our own program managers.

In fact, sailboat racing is its own complete world, demanding from all competitors a total immersion of all their senses and skills into the outcome of each race. And it is virtually impossible to keep this immersion from pervading the sailors' day-to-day lives. Thus you get sailors in church sneaking in a prayer or two for a little help in the frostbiting that afternoon. Or the two 12-year-old junior sailors who, after saying good night to their parents at the dinner party in their home, zigzagged their way across the living room and up the stairs. When asked by a guest about this strange behavior, the parents nonchalantly answered that they were tacking up to bed. Or you find sailors in cars yelling "Up, up, up," and insisting on "room" every time the traffic merges.

The beauty of the sport is that there are so many classes of boats and types of racing that almost everyone can find his or her niche somewhere. And so with so many factors involved in the outcome of every race, the same one rarely determines the winner each time. In fact, sailing is a sport with a lot of specialists who excel with amazing regularity when the conditions are just right for them. In the Soling class there is Sid Dakin, a fellow from Toronto with an uncanny reputation for winning when the wind is extremely light and fluky. And, sure enough, once we were racing Soling on Chesapeake Bay when the wind went completely flat. The water turned glassy and most spinnakers fell draped on the headstalls. One boat, however, managed to keep moving the entire time and went on to win the race, Sid Dakin's. It seem too incredible to be anything but coincidence and good fortune – ah, but that haunting quote, "The winds and currents are always on the side of the ablest navigator."

Okay, so how do we get this ability? Due to a liberal arts education in the social sciences, I have become preoccupied with the offering of equations as solutions to society's problems. So I would like now to offer my equation for understanding the complexity of sailing ability: *Ability = Knowledge + Execution + Attitude.* Knowledge is the sum of all we know about the sport, including our past experiences as well as what we've read and been told; Execution is not what we do to our crew after a bad race, but rather how we actually sail the boat around the course – our boat handling, timing, spinnaker sets, etc.; and Attitude refers to our psyche and mental state – i.e., do we learn from our mistakes, improve every time we go out, remain calm and objective throughout the race, and, most important, have fun doing it?

In the following chapters we'll explore all three areas of the equation, isolating the many factors that go into winning, and focusing on improving each one. We've got a lot to talk about, and to the skeptic it may seem that it is all we ever do. But again, we're dealing with perhaps the most complex sport in the world – and definitely the most fun!

CHAPTER 2

Preparation

*"The good sailors all know how to race very well, but
the champions have won the regatta before the racing begins."*
– Paul Elvström

WHAT! You mean you didn't phone ahead to find out if the motel you're staying in had "Magic Fingers" in the beds? And you don't have a complete set of metric Nico-Press sleeves as well as the standard ones? And you don't even have all the meteorological data taken over the last half year for the area? Don't worry – most sailors don't even stay in motels, much less own a Nico-Press tool, or have more than a clue of how to interpret a half year's data. But as my crew and I focused in on trying to become good enough to make the 1984 U.S. Olympic Team and win a gold medal in Los Angeles, the one fact that became clearer and clearer was that preparation for racing is grossly under-emphasized by the educators in the sport and by most sailors. The reality is that the more we work toward winning, the less and less attention we find ourselves giving to the actual racing, and the more energy and attention we are giving to all the many other elements that fall under the category Preparation.

Now, before I launch into a thesis on the 50 ways to get prepared, let me restate the (sometimes elusive) obvious. Before you start thinking about doing well in sailing, you have to confront the questions: How important is it that you do well in sailing and how much time, money, and energy can you afford to give to the sport? You have to stop and answer these honestly because remarks like this tend to be based on the ideal world where sailors have unlimited time, money, and energy to commit to perfecting their ability; and as there are very few people in that ideal world, the rest of us have to pick and choose what can be applied to our situation. To have an unreal outlook on how racing fits into our lives is the surest way to get nothing but frustration back from the sport.

Another element that keeps a lot of us from being as prepared as possible is our self-consciousness, caused by not wanting to appear too serious about sailing. I can remember when I was racing Lasers hard, and special hiking boots and one-piece foul-weather suits hit the scene. For two years I held on to my Pro-Keds and flannel shirts, thinking that the new clothes were going too far and I could do just fine without them. On the other side you have people who aren't afraid to appear serious, like the winner of two U.S. youth champs, John Shadden, who decided that he and his crew would stay in homes away from the regatta scene in the evenings rather than hang around the crowd. Then there's Peter Commette, who capsized in the opening race of a regatta the spring before he won the first Laser world championship. While the rest of us sat on the beach eating lunch between races, we watched Peter do about 50 jibes out on the course. Everyone's going to have his or her own approach. Again, you have to ask yourself how seriously you want to take sailing and adjust your goals accordingly.

THE FINAL ELEMENT that has always kept me and many other sailors from doing the amount of preparation we should is a combination of laziness and not appreciating how useful good preparation is. Realizing that I had better find out if I could hack the pace of an Olympic Soling campaign before I committed myself and two others to it, I decided to try to do everything I knew I should do in preparation for the worlds in Australia. Though we had the additional element of having to ship our boat down and back, which for most regattas most of us don't have to deal with, we worked on preparations for a few hours nearly every day for the six months leading up to the pre-worlds and worlds.

However, the one thing we couldn't do, because of prior commitments and having to ship the boat three months prior to the regatta, was get together and practice. And though our preparation work paid off well with a second in the pre-worlds and a third in the worlds, our boathandling in the heavy air kept us from winning both. Experiencing that, I now believe that given a good amount of racing knowledge and experience, the largest gains toward winning can be made by shifting your attention and energy to all the elements that go into the preparation for racing.

From here on in this chapter, most of what I'll say has been said by others in more detail, or is purely common sense. But it might make a good outline from which to work.

Speed Preparation

Not many people win regattas going slow, and improving boatspeed should be worked on before the major regattas. It comes in a variety of ways:

- Talk to the top sailors in your area and class.
- Look at the boats and rigs of the top sailors, and incorporate their ideas into your boat.
- Get one of these sailors to sail with you, either in practice, on the way out to a race or, better yet, in a race. Let them steer, then have them watch you.
- Watch races in which the best sailors are racing.
- Mark everything on your boat so you can make notes of where controls are when you're fast and slow.
- **MAKE NOTES OF EVERYTHING**. Sailors who don't make notes of things they learn stand a very poor chance of improving. Also, most good sailors don't mind giving advice once, but most don't have the time or patience to be asked the same question twice.
- The more time you spend sailing the boat, the faster you'll go – period.

Body Preparation

With the exception of a few classes, most of us don't have to get our bodies into the same excellent shape as our boats. But there are some key points to remember:

- Be relaxed so your mind can concentrate. I've heard rumors that a lot of sailors sail their best after a late night of partying. Others have their best races when they're late driving to a regatta, or last off the dock. Apparently these people have to race so fast against traffic and sail so fast to get to the line that they're more prepared and hyped for the race, if they make it. Some enjoy getting away from the scene at night;

others like sleeping down by the clubhouse (probably to be sure no none puts their boat in the club pool). Lately I've noticed I race the best when I've slept well the last three or four nights before the regatta. During regattas, because I get nervous, I don't sleep well, so staying up a bit later usually helps me stay asleep all night. No one races well yawning up the first beat, so get to know your body.

- Stretching really helps you hike and prevents stiffness.

- Good, solid food the night before and lots of water during hot races helps.

- Dress to be comfortable. Being cold is the worst, so when in doubt, overdress. On multiple-race days you get the coldest between races, so bring a wool hat and extra coat for the wait. The extra weight is minimal compared to staying warm.

- Figure out what you're going to do with your wet clothes and laundry so you'll always have dry, clean clothes to race in.

Boat Preparation

Where are all those pit crews you see on TV when you need them? To quote 470 and 505 champion Steve Benjamin on the subject of boat preparation: "There is a simply stated formula for success: attention to detail. Most good sailors agree that boatspeed is derived to a large degree from a meticulous philosophy of improving every minute aspect of the hull and rig. The idea is that if every detail is optimized, regardless of how insignificant, the overall performance should be fully adequate. It's quite easy to stray from this mentality and convince yourself that a small scratch on the bottom could not slow you down, or that you don't use that frozen cleat anyhow, so why bother to fix it. But a true perfectionist will never tolerate such inadequacies and would surely make repairs before the next race of a series."

Here are some things to consider.

- Compile tools, including drill, hacksaw, pop-rivet tool, Nico-Press tool, wire cutters, extension cord, etc. Mark them all clearly as yours.

- Continually rotate and replace lines and wires on the boat. Do every job thoroughly the first time so you won't have to do it again. Ask and if necessary, pay for help.

- When in doubt, copy the fast people, at least for starters.
- Be sure things measure in. Lately I've seen a lot of people thrown off their stride by sails, rudders, spinnaker poles, etc., not measuring in. If possible, have things checked and weighed, including your clothes, before getting to any major regatta.
- Along with the boat, be sure the trailer and car are ready to roll.

Boathandling

This is a key area. Usually the biggest gains and losses on the course are made at the start and at the marks. If I could give only one piece of advice to sailors who are interested in improving their racing, it would be to go out and practice with the same team they usually race with. Isolate each maneuver and work on it alone: setting the pole and taking it down, tacking the jib and main, raising the centerboard, clearing weed, playing the vang on windy reaches, capsizing and recovering, setting the chute, hiking for a mile straight, etc. Boathandling is especially important in high winds, so grab some practice rags and preferably a friend in a motor boat (in case you get in trouble) and go out when it's cranking.

Lists

Lists are another godsend to preparation. They insure that things aren't forgotten and help everyone involved keep in touch with what needs to be done.

ONE OF THE BIG KEYS TO PREPARATION is assigning priorities properly as time begins to run out before each regatta. Too often, people spend three hours sanding their rudder two days before the regatta when they probably would improve their chances of doing well more by going sailing. Priorities will vary for every team, but be sure to ask yourself continually "Is what I'm doing the most important thing to be doing right now?"

From 1978 to 1980 the team of Ed Trevelyan, Rod Davis, and Robbie Haines dominated the U.S. in the Soling and in 1980 were the favorites to win the gold medal had the U.S. sent teams to the Olympics. In a recent talk Robbie called himself an "organizational freak" – "I love to be organized." At regattas their boat always arrived covered; they never showed up late; rarely did they ask to borrow a tool or part; their fund raising was successful enough for good accommodations, good food, and the latest sails and equipment. It's too easy to write this kind of highly successful program off to personal wealth and people with no other commitments. All three of these guys had jobs while they were sailing, one was married, and their funds were all raised through their own efforts. The bottom line to their success was tremendous organization and effort in all the elements of preparation leading up to each regatta. This almost insured that once the racing began, the hardest steps toward winning were already behind them.

Probably the toughest thing to learn as you try to get everything together is that most jobs take five times as long as you had planned and that there are a lot of setbacks along the way. After preparing a Peterson 43 for the 1981 SORC, John Sparkman used to tape the sign "It don't come easy," over the companionway before every race. It served both as a reminder to him of all the work he had done to get the boat ready to race and as one to us, when things were hitting the fan, to do whatever work needed to be done to sail our best. Any sailor who applies that attitude to his preparation for racing will show huge improvements in his finishes immediately.

Crewing

IN THE LAST TWO YEARS I've learned something that, as a skipper, I never really understood – it's damned hard to be a crew. You have to be a contortionist, a psychic, and a glutton for verbal abuse, not to mention flawless. And above all, who reaps the rewards – usually not the crew!

The classic "skipper's mentality" is a need always to be in control. It is overpowering, self-interested, sees itself as infallible and is burdened by the incompetence of people around it. On the other hand, the "crew's mentality" is submissive, passive, almost repulsed by the thought of holding power and, as a result, is tolerant of their subservient position.

Fortunately, most sailors realize that neither of these mentalities is conducive to successful or fun sailing, but unfortunately, most of us – skippers and crews alike – have difficulty overcoming them. The power of these attitudes and the resistance to being forced into an uncomfortable role keep people fighting in the boat, make it difficult for married couples to sail together, and generally keep a team from having fun and reaching its fullest potential.

IT'S IMPERATIVE to channel all of our energy toward the race, and the best way to overcome the negative aspects of skipper and crew mentalities is to confront them. One excellent method is for the skipper and crew to change places for an important race or series early in the summer and seriously try to do as well as possible. While racing, notice the feelings you experience, the frustration, the anger, and the awkwardness and difficulty of doing things you may have previously taken for granted. Above all, talk to each other about how you feel, because it's when the frustration and anger are pent up inside that the spinnaker poles start to fly.

It's well known that no good skipper will sail an important regatta without an equally good crew. The most important underlying attribute of a good crew is that they want to win just as badly as the skipper. For this, it is up to the crew and skipper to psych each other up for the race and to know that, win or lose, they're in it as a team. During the 1977 America's Cup summer, Ted Turner played the inspiring theme from *Rocky* before the big races, and you know those winches started spinning faster!

ANOTHER CRUCIAL ATTRIBUTE that is difficult to achieve is the ability to place the crew's own needs and feelings aside so that they don't interfere with those of the skipper. Here's where the crew must make a sacrifice. They must concentrate hard to get into the mood and flow of the skipper, and be sensitive not to let anything break it. When the skipper is ready to leave the dock, the crew can't be in the bathroom or still putting on foul-weather gear. Details like the spinnaker pole, protest flag, and lunch should be double-checked by the crew, and on the water the crew can't be talking about last night's party if the skipper is trying to evaluate headsails. I never knew there was such an art to this until a close friend, who crewed for me for over two years in a Lightning, told me a little secret. Whenever I felt we were going slow, I'd ask him to let the jib out. But he was good enough to take a look at it himself, and if it looked good, he'd just pop the sheet out of the cleat and then put it right back in the same place. And invariably I'd say, "Ahh, that feels much better."

The next critical attribute is that the crew must become a part of the boat, not like a block or a cleat, but more like a sensitive, thinking extension of the boat as it moves through the water. When they see a puff coming, they should be ready to flatten the boat the instant it begins to heel; likewise, they should be back off the rail when the puff ends so the boat doesn't heel to windward and stall. The same is true for sail trim. For every change in wind, wave, and boatspeed or direction, there should be a corresponding change in sail trim. The good crews will anticipate these without waiting for the skipper. On a reach, as the boat accelerates and the apparent wind shifts forward, the crew should be trimming the jib and/or spinnaker and preparing to ease them again as the boat slows. So often when it looks like someone has better boat speed, it's the result of a hypersensitive crew keeping the boat going at top speed longer than the boats around them.

Finally, the crew must become the eyes of the boat. At the very top levels, the skipper is purely the helmsman, concentrating his total energy on making the boat go fast. It's the crew that looks around, feeds him information, makes decisions, and often calls all the shots. That's how Dave Ullman, two-time 470 World Champion, was beaten by his own crew, Tom Linskey, in the 1978 US SAILING Championship of Champions – two excellent sailors, each with his own specialties and together nearly unbeatable.

Skippers, on the other hand, have to be careful not to stifle and frustrate their crews right out of the boat. A good crew is worth the patience and time it takes to cultivate them. If they don't get the pole up in 0.5 second, don't yell at them. They're probably trying their hardest, and your pressure is just going to slow them down even more. Imagine how you'd feel if you missed a shift and your crew said, "Nice going; you just lost us another five places." Encourage them to talk more, but if some of their judgments are wrong at first, help them to learn and improve.

Finally, the one single thing that would help more people relax, get along better, and dramatically improve their finishing positions is practice. Rounding the windward mark one boatlength ahead of Charlie Archrival is the wrong time to see if your crew can improve on the spinnaker set they completely botched last weekend. Plan to sail at least an hour preceding the weekend race and, if possible, for a few hours during the week. Go through all the maneuvers of tacking, jibing, rounding marks, setting and dousing the spinnaker, and doing two-turn penalties. Let the crew take the helm, let the skipper try to jibe the pole, work out your communication, and eliminate all the bugs in your boathandling and equipment.

Of the equation, *Ability = Knowledge + Execution + Attitude*, most people have more than enough knowledge, but it's their execution that is really weak. Good crew work and practice will make a big difference.

CHAPTER 4

Teamwork

AS THE STORY GOES, there was a husband and wife team who raced very successfully together, except that whenever a situation got tense, the husband, who was the skipper, would start yelling and screaming at his wife. In return, she would calmly tell him that if he didn't shut up she was going to jump overboard and swim away. One day they were racing for the club championship, and coming up to the finish line they were leading the race except for one last starboard tacker. They decided to duck behind it, but at the last second, and with no warning, the husband decided to tack. Needless to say, the crash tack was not picture-perfect and the starboard tacker immediately rolled right over them. The husband started in on his usual condescending yelling at his wife, and with that she calmly stood up and dove overboard, swimming over and climbing onto the nearby race committee boat. Of course, they were scored DNF for that race and thereby lost the championship. Later on that evening at the club bar, the husband was overhead saying, "You know, I really learned something out there I'll never forget..." And as everyone leaned in to finally hear him admit he'd been wrong for treating his wife so poorly, he said, "If I ever get married again, I'm going to find a woman who can't swim."

IN STUDYING PSYCHOLOGY, we learn that people's habits and attitudes are very difficult to change, and that includes our own bad habits on the race course. But we keep trying. One good way to look at our problems is – using my favorite analogy – "to go up in a blimp and look at the total picture." One of the first things we see is that it is counter-productive, when two or more people are in the same boat, for them to have an adversary relationship. All the energy, knowledge, and talent in the boat should be directed toward racing as well as possible. When one person (usually the skipper) starts blaming others for things that go wrong, or starts talking to them in condescending tones of voice, obviously the atmosphere is not going to be pleasant, and as a result the boat's finishing position will be poor.

The best way to avoid anxiety is for everyone on the boat to know what's going on all the time. At the top levels of racing each person in the boat usually can do anyone else's job. Each can skipper pretty well, fly a spinnaker, and handle tactics, so they are able to anticipate situations. In order to help this learning process along on your boat, have everyone take turns doing the other persons' jobs. Sailing out to the race course, the crew should skipper to get more tiller time. This helps them learn how the boat feels, how puffs, waves, and small movements in the boat affect heel, what the sails look like from the back, and also where the crew should sit to avoid blocking the skipper's view of the jib and bow waves. Besides, handing over the tiller is a show of confidence that will build crew confidence and steering a boat is just plain fun to do.

Meanwhile skippers should hike, trim the jib, set the spinnaker, try to jibe the spinnaker, and work to balance the boat just as well as they want their crew to. Often the skipper has more experience and it's much more effective to teach by showing than by telling.

The next step is to keep the roles reversed for a race or a weekend series. Nothing will accelerate the learning curve of inexperienced people more, or help reduce the anxiety level within the boat quicker than this technique. But be sure you do your first role reversals going out to or coming in from a race, or in separate practice sessions. Don't enter a race until everyone is confident in his or her new position.

It's interesting that in the many seminars and regattas I've been to over the years, the proportion of men and women has been very close to 50-50, yet I'd say 90 percent of the skippers are male. If it's lack of confidence on both sides to have the women skippering, then nothing will build confidence more than having the women skipper as much as possible going out to and back in from a race. Very soon their boathandling and feel will be good enough to enter a race, and once they've skippered a few races, their understanding of the whole picture will increase dramatically. You don't build confidence by just talking about it. You have to be active and get more tiller time whenever possible.

ANOTHER GREAT WAY to keep the anxiety level down and the racing performance level up is to talk about who's going to do what before the race begins. You have to be honest and up front about what people's responsibilities are. I'll never forget sailing one of my first big-boat races on a Swan 44 when Bill Ficker, the 1970 America's Cup winner, was the guest skipper. Inasmuch as I didn't know anything about big boats and had even less confidence, my game plan was to volunteer to make sandwiches so I could stay out of the way as much as possible. On the way out to the race, Bill got us all back in the cockpit for a meeting. Never having met us, he asked us what we were good at and then assigned each person specific things to do. I ended up trimming the mainsheet at the start, during tacks and at mark roundings, grinding for the spinnaker sheet trimmer on the reaches, and watching for other boats upwind. I got totally involved and learned a great deal.

Also, during a race it's often difficult to explain everything that's going on, but after the race it's vital that everyone on the boat sit together and go over what just happened. A lot can be learned in a brief 20-minute review session, and this is especially helpful to less experienced members of the crew who are really interested in learning. Most people who are psyched to learn are aware that they don't know everything, so they're prepared to hear criticism and comments on how to improve. The worst attitude is the "I know" syndrome, where it's impossible to give a person a suggestion. A chain is only as strong as its weakest link, and if one member of the team (either skipper or crew) hides in an "I know it all" shell and won't listen to constructive suggestions, the team will never gel and reach its potential.

IT'S ALSO VITAL to discuss what sort of communication the skipper wants during the race. Personally, 30 seconds before the start I want to know how close to the line we are, if there are any boats threatening to take our hole to leeward, what the time is, etc. Immediately after the start the only things I want to know are what our relative boatspeed is, how we are pointing, who is directly to windward and leeward (different people have different sailing styles), how much room to leeward I have to play with, and whether I can tack or not. The key to giving information is to make sure that everything you say is useful. If you're on a collision course with someone before the start,

Report relative boat speed in two dimensions: One is fore-and-aft speed on a line parallel to your course; the other is "height," i.e., if they are a leeward boat, are they getting closer to you or are they dropping away farther to leeward?

don't say, "Hey, look out for the boat up there." Instead say, "Do you see the blue boat, Number 322?" And after the start, comments like "Man, that guy is motoring on us over there" can earn you a quick boom crutch in the teeth. The reason is that such a comment has no useful information in it. Factual reports like, "There's a boat ten boatlengths to windward that is pointing higher, but they've got a puff which we should get in about 30 seconds," is the kind of info that a skipper can use. Also, in terms of relative boatspeeds, I like to think in two dimensions: fore-and-aft speed along a line parallel to me; and height, i.e. are they dropping in on us or are they moving away to windward (see diagram).

As you get more experienced, you can tell if a boat is gaining or losing; and in giving boatspeed feedback I always talk about our boat to avoid any confusion. So a conversation might be, "There's a boat to windward – we're lower (meaning we're dropping more to leeward) but faster (meaning we're moving faster in a fore and aft direction). I think the net gain is to us." Or, "There's a boat to windward – we're higher but slower. They're definitely gaining on us." This info tells the skipper whether to pinch or foot more, and to either keep all controls where they are or make some adjustments. A comment like "The windward mark is about half a mile up at two o'clock, just to the left of a large, green spinnaker" gives the skipper a lot of references so all it takes is a quick look to find the mark. Good meaty info like this will help keep the energy flow directed on the racing and reduce the anxiety within the boat. The bottom line is that the more you are allowed to give information, the better you'll get at giving it. No one will be perfect the first few times, but you have to take action and start doing it to get good at it.

In an interview I did for the U.S. Olympic Yachting Committee's publication *Pipeline*, three Olympic caliber sailors talked about their experiences as crews in serious campaigns. They were Ed Trevelyan, 1979 world champion and 1980 Olympic Trials winner in Solings sailing with Robbie Haines and Rod Davis; Neal Fowler, 1980 470 Olympic Trials winner sailing with Steve Benjamin; and Jay Glaser, 1981 Tornado world champion sailing with Randy Smyth. Here are some excerpts:

Q: What was your role while racing?

NEAL: With Benj, initially I was calling almost every move, and Benj just drove like a maniac. This was fine until we lost the '79 Midwinters in a big way. We then went into the feed system (where the crew feeds info to the skipper continuously). This is far and away the best. We both know everything, no surprise moves. If either felt strongly about something, he just raised his voice and that was that. If there was not enough time for discussion and I was not sure, Benj just went into the maneuver. I could tell by the motion of the boat what needed to be done.

Q: What are some of the hardest things about being a crew?

JAY: The difficult things about crewing are mental. One for me is lack of recognition and identity. It can be a project in which the crew contributes 50 percent of the effort in funds, talent, time, etc., but the team is always identified with the driver. I was "Richard's crew" (past Tornado National Champion Richard Loufek), and now I'm "Randy's crew" to a lot of the sailors who know us. However, among the crews themselves there is some recognition, and I have my own crew heroes – those crews who by their sheer talent can pull drivers to the front of the fleet.

Q: What are the positive things about crewing?

ED: The satisfaction of getting the teamwork down to a level where most of the functions are automatic. Rod and I couldn't wait to get on somebody's tail at the wing mark in 20 to 25 knots so we could do that perfect jibe we had practiced so much. Also, there was the satisfaction of knowing that I was an integral part of our campaign, as were Rod and Robbie, and not just ballast for the almighty skipper. I felt at the beginning that it would be fun to crew because the big pressures of skippering would not be there. This was not the case; I was always nervous before a big race because I knew it was essentially up to me to figure out the windshifts, etc. The same went for Rod in his functions. So when we won I got a real sense of accomplishment even though I was "just a crew".

JAY: A positive point of crewing is working well with a driver and having your efforts rewarded. Randy and I put a lot of time into fitness programs, practice and regattas. It paid off with a win at the worlds. Another positive point is that crewing enables me to compete successfully at a level I couldn't as a driver. If you bought a Stradivarius violin and practiced hard for ten years you still might not be first chair in the symphony orchestra. Some people are natural drivers. My solution was to be the best crew possible and sail with Richard and Randy. In the same way, due to temperament or whatever, some are more natural crews.

FROM OUR BLIMP, it's clear to see that the boats up front are filled with people working together to get the most out of their boat and themselves and that the farther back in the fleet you get, the more you see arguments, skippers yelling orders at their crews, and crews taking passive roles in the boat. One of the most valuable skills of a good skipper is the ability to remain patient when training a new crew. A good crew is well worth the time and energy it takes to cultivate him or them, and nothing will turn away a potential teammate faster than a continual barrage of abuse. Next time you go racing, take a quick trip in the blimp and see what the interaction in your boat looks like.

CHAPTER 5

The Quest for Gold

IT IS ALMOST IMPOSSIBLE to imagine the fanatical level of preparation a sailor goes through in a serious Olympic campaign. The first and most important step is that all sailors who are going for it have decided that they can win the Trials if they put in the necessary time and work. This forms the basis for the incredible competition, as there always seem to be at least four or five teams who feel they can win. And then the fun begins!

Starting way back at the previous Trials, each sailor tries to outdo his opponents in every area imaginable. Most contenders have gone through at least one and sometimes two boats in the past four years, before arriving at the one they will race in the Trials. Hyper-attention is paid to the critical strength vs. weight ratio, and every avenue allowable by the rules is explored. Most of these sailors have partially or completely built their own boats to be sure that every rib is in the perfect place, every excess ounce of resin and glass is removed, and every piece of wood used has been properly chosen and cured.

Then there is the secrecy. Most sailors are extremely guarded about what has gone into their boats, and justifiably so. All the top Olympic contenders are intelligent and creative sailors who have spent the last four years thinking about little else than how to improve their chances to win; and to be sure, all of them have made improvements in the hulls that will be an advantage. But because it is nearly impossible to get in and see what's been done once the boats have been put together, the sailors use this for a little psychological warfare. Just planting the notion in your opponents' minds that you've made an improvement on your boat is often enough to drive them crazy, until either they have decided it's not an improvement after all, or have figured out how to do it to their boats.

This technological and psychological warfare goes on in every area of the effort – masts, booms, hardware, trailers, shipping covers, and support boats. One top crew in the Flying Dutchman class some years ago was simultaneously finishing his last year at med school, but instead of reading and study-ing at a desk, he rigged up a home trapeze system in his living room complete with counterweights. He even wore his weight jacket to simulate the actual racing conditions as closely as possible.

In the Tornado class, a highly sensitive scale is one of their most impor-tant tools, and each sailor could tell you down to the ounce what every fit-ting on the boat weighs. The Finn boys are heavily into their diets and spend their evenings mixing milk shakes filled with powdered protein and vitamin and mineral additives, not to mention bananas, eggs, and gobs of ice cream.

When you get to a Soling or Star regatta, attention in the parking lot goes to the most obvious topic: the rudder, keel and hull fairness. "Hey, check out this guy's trailing edge; looks like he's built it up about an eighth of an inch – – looks fast!" "This boat looks like it's been painted. I wonder if he's tweaked the tolerances anywhere?" It's also important to check out what substances people put on their bottoms prior to racing. Industrial soaps are very popu-lar, as are Teflon lubricants. Some are applied with a spongy brush, others from aerosol spray guns. And about the only thing you can say for sure is that everyone's got something a little different – once again, just working away on that crucial psychological advantage.

In most of the top Olympic campaigns, the sailors spend three times as much time working on their boats as they do sailing them! This is staggering when you consider that the top contenders have averaged close to four or five hours of sailing a day twice a week. Of course, these periods of sailing are grouped together, so that they might spend a solid month sailing five hours a day, seven days a week and then take a month or so off to build a new boat. Also, rarely a day goes by when they're not doing some sort of work for their boats, and the lists of things to do seem endless.

TIME ON THE WATER is taken very seriously and is spent in three areas: boathandling techniques – roll tacking, jibing, spinnaker work, rounding marks, ducking boats; sailing techniques – steering waves, coordinating skip-per and crew movements for ooching and pumping, and learning more about the exact balance of the boat; and, of course, boatspeed. Boatspeed testing is generally done with one or two other boats and involves sailing for long distances, making small changes, and sailing some more. Most racers have a sail loft worth of sails in their vans, and the process of reconciling all the variables, including differences between the helmsmen and crews (so that you can get an accurate reading from the different sails) is a long one.

As you must imagine, the question of how the sailors support themselves becomes critical in an Olympic campaign, and there is no question that funding is a determining factor in the success of any program. Sailors involved in serious Olympic campaigns have decided that it is the most important thing to them at that time in their lives. In this commitment, they've joined the thousands of other American athletes who have put aside their schooling, their job opportunities, and all other commitments to try for the Olympic games. And the athletes are dependent, to a small degree, on their national organization and, to the largest degree, on themselves to raise the money.

Unfortunately, sailing at the Olympic level is expensive. Besides the costs of the hull, sails, and equipment, you have the cost of traveling, living, entry fees, insurance premiums, etc. Most of the funds are raised through personal appeals to individuals who can make tax-deductible contributions to the United States Sailing Foundation (USSF). Often a yacht club will make a contribution to its own Olympic aspirants. Many of the top contenders are in the sailing industry by profession and can write off much of their effort. Others not in the profession are often given aid in the way of discounts and delayed payment terms. Several of the top contenders have worked hard over the past few years to earn their own money, and some continue to work while they are training, slipping in sailing time before and after work. In short, figuring out how to support themselves during an Olympic effort requires as much attention as the actual racing does.

The important thing to remember is this: although only one team will go on to the games in each class, everyone who has made the effort to get to the Olympics comes out a winner. The Olympics represent an extremely concrete, short-term and highly competitive goal with a narrow and clearly defined path leading to it. And for those who have chosen to try, the experience of putting all their effort, skill, time, and energy toward one goal is rewarding in itself.

Along the way, each sailor travels around the country and the world. In only one year, sailors at the Trials will have been to England, France, Spain,

Italy, Holland, Denmark, Norway, Sweden, Finland, German, Russia, Japan, New Zealand, Australia, South Africa, Brazil, Mexico, Puerto Rico, Canada, and almost every sailing area in the U.S.! They will have made friends with people throughout the world, and they will have grown extremely close to the sailors they are traveling with and competing against.

In addition, through their own personal efforts they will have directly caused the further advancement and improvement of the sport of sailboat racing. Through their research and testing work with the major sailing industries, large steps have been taken in recent years. We are now working closer than ever with the aeronautical industries, resulting in better materials and construction techniques. New sail materials are now available in some classes, which should provide lighter and longer-lasting sails during the nineties. And through the constant exposure of our Olympic hopefuls in the magazines, at the regattas, and during seminars, more and more of our young sailors are getting turned on to sailing at a higher level than ever before.

Also, not only will these Olympic hopefuls have dramatically improved their skills and understanding of racing sailboats but, more important, they will have learned the skills and the value of organization, of cooperation, of preparation, of understanding their own mental and physical strengths and weaknesses, and how to deal with a highly competitive and pressurized situation. But perhaps the greatest lesson of the whole trip is learned when it's all over – how to deal with failure, the bitter disappointment that is inevitable for all but one of the many teams who dedicated the last two or four years of their lives entirely and solely toward this one regatta.

The whole picture considered, the group of sailors who line up at the U.S. Olympic Selection Trials is not your ordinary fleet of sailors. They are a remarkable collection of talented, determined, imaginative, and hard-working athletes who pull out all the stops in their dual effort to win the right to represent the U.S. at the Summer Olympic Games and to prove to themselves that they were able to overcome all the obstacles along the way; and to pull it all together when they had to.

CHAPTER 6

Helping

IN JULY 1979, I attended a seminar sponsored by the Ontario Sailing Association in Finns, and the guest expert was Paul Elvström. On the first day of sailing, 20 Finns hit the water, followed by the drill leader's boat, two crash boats, several marks, and Elvström in a separate coach's boat loaded with videotaping equipment, recorders, and loud-hailers. After an extremely busy morning of speed testing, boathandling drills, and mark-rounding practice, the group ate lunch and then gathered around the videotape playback set. What followed was a fascinating and eye-opening insight into an area of the sport that people are just beginning to explore, yet one that is critical to the continuation and advancement in the techniques of sailboat racing.

On the screen we were watching a Finn being sailed upwind. The camera was focused on the motion of the rudder, the wake as it left the hull and rudder, the angle of heel, and the hiking posture of the skipper. Elvström was explaining, "The natural tendency of the Finn is to head up, and so it is important to keep it very flat. Also, with such a large rudder, you must be careful not to oversteer. Oh – and look! Stop the film. When that puff hit, the boat heeled slightly, and you can see the imbalance of the wake as the rudder stalled out."

The response to his criticism was usually the same: "It's amazing. I thought I had been keeping it flat, but I can see clearly that I was nowhere near flat. And whenever I've felt stalled, I've bounced the boat like a Laser, but I can see that that technique just randomly opens and closes my leech, which is probably what's hurting my pointing ability."

Since the beginning, sailing has been an individualistic sport, with people working extremely hard on their own boatspeed, boathandling, and tactical knowledge. Unfortunately, this has given rise to a small handful of excellent sailors in each class who now dominate the class championships. These are the people who can afford the time and luxury to continually think about and practice their art. But for the rest, sailing must take its place alongside the family, career, and other responsibilities, thereby limiting the chance that they will ever reach their full potential on their own.

THE NEXT STEP, then, is for people to work together to help each other improve. Unfortunately, many people find it very difficult to share their knowledge, trying to cling to any small advantage they can. Often, this knowledge is incomplete and inaccurate; besides, racing is definitely most fun and most challenging when most of the people racing can sail well enough to have a good shot at winning.

Here, then, are several ways people can help each other get more out of the sport of sailing. When training for the Olympics, most serious contenders will team up with at least one other contender with whom they'll test speed, discuss new ideas, and generally push hard against. This same principle can apply to all levels of the sport. Find someone you like and respect, preferably one who is a little better than you, and go sailing together. When speed testing, go upwind on both tacks, and give both boats the chance to be leeward boat. Determine who is faster, have that boat remain constant, and make changes in the other boat until both are going at the same speed and pointing equally. It's extremely helpful for the two skippers to switch boats, but the crews should stay in their own boats. When sailing this way, stay close together, and continually watch the compass, as a shift in the wind will benefit one of the boats.

For the boathandling practice, use buoys. It's unrealistic and misleading to practice heavy air jibes around imaginary marks. Besides, fixed marks give instant feedback on your rounding. Start with one boat behind the other and have tacking duels upwind and jibing duels downwind. Stop frequently to discuss techniques and to watch each other's boathandling maneuvers. If you are watching more than one boat at a time, you can provide a comparative analysis. Just see which boats are tacking better and tell the others what they are doing that's different.

The extension of this is to have a coach. A coach is someone whose job it is to help you improve and race as well as possible. He or she can be a better sailor or someone you import from the outside. Of course, someone has to organize the practice so that the coach has time to get together with the sailors, and this rarely gets done. But people who have been well coached know the incredible effect it has on their ability and overall awareness in the sport.

Good coaches will emphasize learning. They'll understand that different people will have different hang-ups and be patient with everyone. They'll use drills to concentrate on boathandling. For instance, they'll have all boats start on starboard tack. Then, when a horn or whistle is heard, everyone will have to tack. This is repeated five or six times. The sailors who are tacking better will quickly move to the front. The sailors in back can then stop and watch the better tackers, and the coach can provide a comparative analysis. This also works well with stopping on one horn and accelerating on the next, bearing off and jibing, two-turn penalties, etc. The best feature, besides being fun, is that the entire fleet is improving together, resulting in better racing and, ultimately, better sailors.

The coach can also sit on the starting line, on the beats and at the marks, suggesting tactics, pointing out mistakes, and reminding people of the rules. Whenever possible, the coach should hop in a boat and race against the sailors. The coach can put the sailors in tough positions, point out offensive and defensive moves as they're happening, and sharpen the crews with whom the sailors are sailing. And as they probably won't win every race, they can really get the others more psyched up to try hard.

Perhaps the best way people can help others is to help them relax. Too often, anxious parents, instructors, and coaches instill a fear of losing into their sailors, making them incredibly uptight and nervous before racing. If you feel this pressure yourself, just let your parent or instructor know. If you have an effect on others, be sure they know how you feel. Your primary concern is that they try their hardest and have a good time. Over-pressuring and over-coaching usually lead to over-trying and poor race results.

Finally, sailors can greatly help each other at regattas. Besides the usual help of unloading boats and buying the first round of beer, the better, more experienced sailors can help those less experienced to improve. At one of the Laser Nationals we held what we called a "Winner's Roast" after the first two days of racing. After dinner, over 150 of the 200 registrants got together, and the winners of each of the day's races stood up and told how they did it. They then answered questions and comments from other competitors. This went on for two hours each night. Besides being really fun, the Winner's Roast was a huge step toward closing the gap between the top sailors and the less experienced, which can only result in better racing for everyone.

THE KEY to all of this is achieving a broader awareness of our ability and learning where our strengths and weaknesses lie. We can only go so far on our own, and the learning curve for most people who have been serious about sailing for more than four or five years becomes very gradual. Remember, you can't begin to learn until you admit to yourself that there are things you don't know. The next big step won't come with the purchase of a new suit of sails or a new boat – it will only come from the help of other people and from your wanting to learn.

So get together with some friends and go out and practice. Offer to help others in your fleet and club by giving talks or running drills. Arrange for top sailors to give seminars and sail in your regattas. Even look into renting or borrowing some videotape equipment to use for a day at your club. All of these things, and more, will allow you and others to get much more out of sailing, have a better time, and send your learning curve spiraling toward levels it couldn't have reached on its own.

Developing Boatspeed

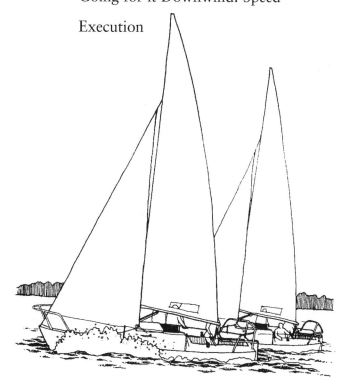

The Language of Speed

SUMMER SAILING is real close, and you have a case-of-beer bet with your best friend that this is the season you're going to put it all together and win everything in sight. You remember hearing someone say once, "Give me a half-a-knot edge in boatspeed, and I'll make you think I'm the smartest guy out there." Ooooo, what you'd do for that half a knot! Well, to get it, you have to work at it, and to do that effectively, you have to know the language. So this chapter is written for people like me who have trouble remembering everything that happens when you ease the backstay, tighten the vang, or sag the jib luff. I've tried to hit most of the controls you might have at your disposal, and simply explain what they do, and what effect they have on other things.

Mainsail-Related Controls

MAINSHEET In addition to its obvious function, the mainsheet controls the tension on the main leech, which determines how much the sail will twist. Pulling on the leech also bends the mast aft.

HALYARD In addition to its obvious function of pulling the main up, the main halyard has several other effects: 1) Easing it decreases the luff tension at the top of the sail, opening the leech and flattening the top of the sail; 2) Pulling it up tighter has the opposite effect; 3) A tight halyard can cause compression in the mast (if a masthead halyard lock is not used); 4) The halyard also adds weight aloft, so care must be taken to use as small a shackle and wire diameter as you safely can; 5) If the halyard is external it adds windage as well. (Finn sailors use a thin object, such as a batten, to push their external halyard inside their sail-track groove.) 6) If the halyard is a loosely woven line, be sure to pull all the stretch out when you first hoist and cleat it.

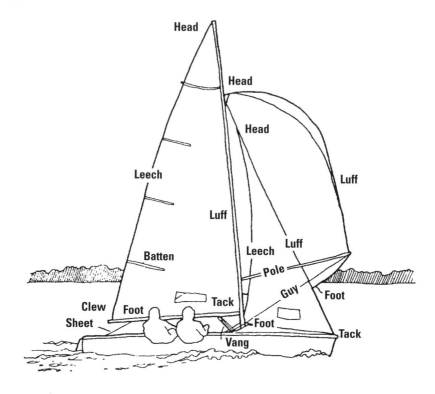

DOWNHAUL The main downhaul is often called the cunningham. Pulling down on it puts tension on the luff, which causes the draft (the name for the deepest part of the sail) to move forward in the sail toward the luff. As the draft moves forward, the top of the leech (in the area of the top batten) will open up. (Notice that this is different from pulling up on the halyard, which closes the top of the leech.) Making the sail flatter or fuller is not the primary job of the downhaul; primarily it positions the draft in the sail. Easing the downhaul lets the draft go back toward the leech, causing the front of the sail to become flatter and the leech tighter. When the draft gets farther back than the sailmaker designed it to be, horizontal wrinkles will appear along the luff.

OUTHAUL Pulling out on the outhaul stretches the cloth between the tack and the clew. This causes the bottom portion of the sail to become flatter. It also causes the leech in the area of the lower battens to open up. Some sails are built with a lens or shelf foot, which permits the sail to become very flat when the outhaul is pulled tight and very full when it is eased. On loose-foot-ed mainsails (e.g. on a Laser) the outhaul works much the same way.

VANG The vang's main purpose is to control the leech of the main– the tighter it is, the tighter the leech. The vang also affects mastbend: if it is attached from the boom to the mast, then it simply pulls the boom down, tightening the leech, which in turn bends the upper section of the mast; if the vang goes from the boom to the deck behind the mast, then when tightened it tries to push the boom forward into the mast, causing the lower section to bend if not otherwise restricted.

MAIN TRAVELER Dropping the main traveler to leeward turns the entire main away from the wind, depowering the sailplan for windier conditions. In light air, when the sheet is eased, pulling the traveler to windward will help center the boom. In some classes the traveler has been eliminated as too cumbersome and heavy. Instead, the vang is used to adjust the leech tension, and the sheet simply controls the in and out portion of the boom.

BATTENS The battens should be as long as class rules permit and should fit so snugly into the pockets that they are difficult to get in and out; this supports the leech and keeps it straight. The flimsier the batten, the more the leech will curl; the stiffer, the straighter it will stay.

LEECH LINE The leech line is a thin cord inside the leech tape (back edge) of the sail. It keeps the leech tape from fluttering as the breeze increases. If pulled too tight in light air, the leech tape will hook over.

Jib-Related Controls

HEADSTAY ATTACHMENT Traditionally, a jib is attached to a permanent headstay using hanks (or snaps, snap hooks, twist hooks, etc.), which makes it easy to lower the jib (it won't fall in the water). An alternative system is for the sailmaker to sew a second wire inside the luff that will act as another headstay, an approach that provides less windage (with few or no hanks) and lets us use a very thin wire for the regular permanent headstay to simply hold up the mast at the dock. In some classes, common practice is to stuff another headstay down inside the luff before every race. An advantage of these latter systems, if the permanent headstay is adjustable, is that the permanent headstay can be pulled tighter than the headstay inside the jib luff, and thereby sag the jib luff to leeward when we need to. Sag in the jib luff makes the sail fuller, the draft moves forward, and the leech opens up. The opposite is true when the luff is tightened. Often, when sagged, the jib will rotate with the leech ending up closer to the mainstay thereby narrowing the slot between the main and the jib.

HALYARD If the wire that is your headstay is sewn into the jib, then your halyard can control your rake. (Rake is simply the amount the mast leans forward to back in the boat.) Pull the halyard tighter and you rake the mast forward; ease it and the mast goes aft. On the other hand, if the cloth of the luff is hanked on the permanent headstay, then the halyard affects jib shape as the main halyard affects the main.

TACK DOWNHAUL This is the jib's downhaul, and it has the same effect as the main's. Many boats don't have this adjustment, but do have the head and tack of the jib simply tied off, so be sure to adjust the tension on both of these before the race begins. Also, sliding the entire jib up the headstay does the same thing as moving the jib lead forward, i.e. it makes the jib fuller and the leech tighter; lowering it does the opposite.

JIB SHEET AND JIB LEADS The jib leads control the general shape of the jib, and the jib sheet tension controls the degree to which you alter that general shape. As you move the jib lead forward, the jib sheet pulls down more on the leech (making it tighter) and less on the foot (making the lower part of the sail fuller – similar to the main outhaul). Moving the jib leads aft does the opposite. Moving the lead inboard or outboard with a barber hauler narrows or widens the slot between the jib and the main.

Spinnaker-Related Controls

HALYARD Pulling the halyard right to the top keeps the chute from swinging around and becoming unstable, and usually exposes more area. In some instances a slightly eased halyard may open up the slot between the jib and spinnaker or may keep the head free of jumpers and other rigging aloft.

SHEET LEAD The sheet lead position has the same effect on the fullness of the foot and on the leech tension as the jib sheet lead. Notice that when the sheet is under the boom, the boom itself becomes the effective lead position, making the sail fuller and the leech tighter. When the sheet is carried over the boom, it has the opposite effect.

GUY LEAD The guy is what we call the spinnaker sheet that goes through the end of the pole, so the end of the pole is the guy lead. The pole height is controlled by the topping lift (pole uphaul) and either a foreguy (pole downhaul) or a guyhook system. Adjusting the pole height changes the height of the spinnaker tack (the clew that has the guy attached to it), which controls the tension on the luff, the overall shape of the chute, and the leech. As the tack is lowered, the luff gets tighter, the chute gets fuller, and the leech opens. As the clew is raised, the luff loosens, the chute gets flatter, and the leech tightens.

Other Areas Where You Have Control

CLASS RULES It's important that your boat be optimized, i.e. maximum height and distance for all sail measurement bands on mast and boom, maximum length pole, full height of jib and spinnaker halyard sheaves, etc.

SIDE SHROUDS Some boats have no side shrouds, others have a complex web of them. Basically, the mast tries to fall over to leeward and the side shrouds support it. They exert a force in the direction of the straight line between where they're attached to the mast and where they next intersect something, i.e. at the end of a spreader or at the deck. The strength of the force they exert is determined by their tension. If they intersect the deck aft of the mast, then they pull the mast back against the headstay, making the headstay tighter.

SPREADER Spreaders are very versatile and important mast controls. They allow shrouds attached to the mast above them to be extended farther outboard before turning downward to the deck, which increases the force each shroud exerts in restricting the top of the mast from falling sideways. Spreaders also exert a force into the mast at the point where they're attached.

Mastbend Controls and What They Do

A MAST can be bent or kept from bending in a variety of ways, depending on the shroud tension and angle, spreader lengths and angles, mast construction, and controls. Also, a mast can be bent fore and aft and sideways; and down low, in the middle, or up top. Each has a different effect on the sailplan of the boat. It is impossible to list and describe all the possible shroud and spreader combinations in this space, but as an example, if the spreaders are cocked aft and the shrouds pulled tight, they will be pushing the middle of the mast forward. If the headstay intersects the mast below the intersect point of the shrouds, the mast will be encouraged to bend forward even more. And if the spreaders go straight out from the mast and the lower shrouds leave the mast right below the spreaders and intersect the deck behind the mast, the middle bend of the mast will be restricted.

PERMANENT BACKSTAY This is led from the tip of the mast to the transom and is usually adjustable. When you tighten it, the tip of the mast is pulled aft, inducing middle to upper mastbend. Bending the mast flattens the main in the area of the bend and causes the draft to move aft. It also pulls the jib halyard sheave aft, tightening the headstay, and it shortens the distance between the head and clew of the main, which opens the leech.

DECK, MASTBEND CONTROLS Mast blocks, lines around the mast, levers, rams, pushers, etc., are all controls at the deck used to control mastbend on a mast stepped through the deck. If, for instance, you put all your mast blocks in front of the mast and pull your backstay, the tip of the mast will go aft, but the blocks will restrain the middle and lower sections from going forward. This will result in a tighter headstay without the lower sections of the main becoming flatter. Of course the main leech will twist open more, requiring mainsheet tension to retain the same shape. In light air, loading mast blocks behind the mast (or adjusting your mast puller) forces the mast to bend (this is called prebend). This will enable a boat without a backstay to get a flatter main shape without ending up with too tight a leech. For masts stepped on deck, cutting away a section of the step, or using a shim will affect the mastbend. For instance, cutting away the front edge of the mast base, or shimming the aft edge, will encourage the mast to bend forward more. The opposite will act to restrict it.

HAVING READ THIS, go out to your boat and see how it's set up. How are the spreaders angled, where do the shrouds intersect the mast, what sort of mastbend controls do you have, how is your jib attached to your headstay, etc.? Then get a copy of the class rules. Are your bands at maximum points, does the class prohibit adjustable headstays or mast levers, etc.? Finally, put up the sails and go sailing; lie on your back, look up at your main and jib, and have a friend begin making adjustments. Move around in the boat, or get onto a powerboat, and look at the leeches, the mastbend (fore and aft and sideways) and the slot. If you know your own boat, it will be very much easier to make comparative analyses of others, and to ask more meaningful questions of your sailmaker or class expert. And it's a lot more fun when you can understand their language, especially since you'll then be better equipped to find that elusive extra half knot of boatspeed.

CHAPTER 8

Those Lovely Light Air Days

RACING IN LIGHT AIR requires the same approach as racing in heavy: You have to like it to do well. To me, the only good thing about racing in light air is that you can usually sail barefoot. But statistics show that over 75 percent of all races in the U.S. are sailed in less than ten knots, so I'm working on adjusting my attitude.

There's no doubt that it is tough to do well in a race in light air and it is tactically very challenging. In heavy air the good boathandlers and hard hikers quickly move to the front, while in light air most people can make the boat go, keeping the fleet much tighter around the course. The boats lose more speed with each turn, so tacks and jibes, etc., must be used more sparingly. Wind shadows extend much farther downwind. And the wind can be a lot crazier, making it even more important, but trickier, to be in the right place at the right time.

Let's look at light air boatspeed first. Again, as in heavy air, each boat will have its particular tuning and sailing characteristics, and it's smart to talk with the best sailors in your class and to look over their boats. But there are plenty of general rules that will apply to sailing all boats in light air. The first is to recognize that every boat carries its own wind. For example, the faster the boat goes upwind, the stronger the breeze blowing on the boat will feel. This stronger wind (apparent wind) will be shifted more toward the bow than the actual wind. In five knots of breeze a boat that has been sailing at four knots for two minutes may have an apparent wind velocity of eight knots, while a boat that has just tacked may only have an apparent wind of six knots. Therefore, two boats side by side can be sailing in much different wind strengths and at different angles. So the bottom line in light air is to always sail for speed. Foot more upwind (increased speed also increases the lift on the board or keel, resulting in less side slipping), reach up higher downwind and make your turns smooth and long when tacking, jibing, and rounding marks.

Also, because true wind varies so much in different parts of the course on a light air day, thinking speed should cause you to change your tactic in order to search out the best breeze available. For example, when the fleet is tightly packed at the start, the wind tends to become lighter because it lifts up over the bulk of the group. So starting near the left end on starboard or near the right end and tacking quickly to port, usually gets you into the clearest wind. Cutting back into the middle across a lot of transoms soon after the start leads you into a jungle of disturbed air and wakes. Another advantage of staying to a side of the fleet is that puffs come in across the course very slowly, which means that the boats on the side the puffs come in from get them and keep them longer, exaggerating the advantage gained. On a boat-for-boat basis, if a boat tacks in front of you in light air, there is a delay before the air it's now disturbing gets to you. This gives you time to decide whether to foot off to leeward of their wind shadow, or tack. And downwind it's critical that you continually look at your telltales or masthead fly to see where your wind is coming from, and then look around to see if another boat is interfering with your wind source. If one is, then head up, bear off, or jibe to clear your air.

TO SET THE SAILS, the best advice again is to check with the fast people in your class; but in general the sails should be set to the topography of the water. If the water is smooth, then flat lower sections and medium-open leeches go well. Experiment with keeping your outhaul tighter than you might think and moving your jib leads aft. Move the draft aft by easing the downhaul and/or bending the mast slightly. The latter also keeps a bit of headstay tension, keeping the jib's draft from creeping too far forward. Try different amounts of jib and mainsheet tensions. The telltales on the jib should both be streaming aft with the inside (windward) one lifting occasionally.

In light and lumpy conditions (the worst!) full lower sections and open leeches go well. Ease the outhaul and jib leads forward. Ease the backstay so the main is full and jib sags some, creating a fuller, more draft-forward shape. Ease the sheets and drive. In these conditions, the jib telltales should be stream-

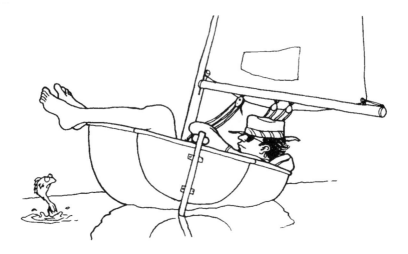

ing, with the outside (leeward) one lifting occasionally as you drive off for more speed.

Sometimes in very light air the sheer weight of the boom puts too much leech tension on the main. Holding the boom up with your arm or (preferably) something else, opens the leech nicely. On the Soling we attached the spinnaker halyard and topping lift to either side of the boom back by the mainsheet bale, taking up on the windward one and easing the leeward one when we tacked. Also, the crew can often handhold the clew of the jib to adjust the fullness of the foot and tension on the leech. The key is to encourage as much wind to flow over the sails and through the slot as fast as possible. Getting things too tight and closed is the quickest way into the parking lot.

When possible, the boom should be on or near centerline, which means pulling the traveler up to windward. One of the crew should constantly check to be sure the boom is centered, and, if possible, on each tack the crew should "tack" the traveler so the boom remains centered.

When it comes time to tack or jibe, the boat should be rolled so a minimum of speed and momentum are lost. In a tack, turn the tiller very slightly, use your weight to help turn the boat (remember heeling to the left turns the boat to the right), and come out of the tack driving off an extra five degrees with sails eased until full speed is reached; then come up to close-hauled. Keeping a bit of heel to leeward after the tack helps the boat accelerate. In very light air, often the turn of a tack causes the apparent wind to keep shift-ing right around too so that it appears you've gotten a huge lift just as you start to tack. In general, stop your turn after you've gone about 95 degrees, and wait for the apparent wind to settle down and reattach.

In a jibe, again turn slowly and smoothly. Bring the main in so it's 45 degrees off centerline. Roll the boat hard to windward to help turn it to lee-ward. Just as the stern crosses the wind, pull the main over hard and fast and let it out to 45 degrees again, reaching up extra high for speed. When full speed is reached, bear off to your course, easing your main.

If you're sailing close-hauled and get a lift, it's usually faster to ease your sails first, then heel the boat slightly to leeward and head up. Often if it's very light and shifty, you may choose just to play the sails and not turn the boat at all. Every time you turn the rudder and the boat you lose speed and momen-tum. Also if you're going close astern of another boat, remember that the wind will momentarily lift across its transom. Though you probably won't want to head up in the brief lift, you should definitely ease your sails in it.

Dead downwind, sit together and far forward. Keep the boat level or slightly heeled to windward. Tie the boom out if needed. Pull your mast for-ward with either your adjustable forestay (if you have one) or with a line tied from your mast around the forestay and back to the mast. This also keeps the rig from shaking around. Pull your board up almost all the way. If you have the chute up, be sure to use light sheets so the chute will lift. Also, keep the pole lowered to help the chute fill. If necessary, be sure someone holds the sheet up out of the water so it doesn't drag. Because the jib breaks the flow of air into the chute, it's important to get it down as quickly as possible, or at least tie it up to the forestay. Ideally you should be dropping the jib as you raise the chute. Uncleating the halyard and simply standing on the tail is a quick way for the person hoisting the chute to control the precise drop of the jib. If you can't drop it or if you plan to leave it up, at least be sure it's almost luffing as you set the chute. The chute will pop full sooner and then the jib can be trimmed back in.

When you're sailing dead downwind, especially with a spinnaker, it's usu-ally better to reach up for speed. Keeping the apparent wind angle at about 100 to 120 degrees aft seems to be the fastest course for most boats. The game is to reach up, build speed and then, as your apparent wind shifts forward, bear off with it. In this way you can keep your pole near your headstay and still make progress toward the leeward mark. As your speed drops and the wind shifts aft, reach up again. Often boats will jibe through 90 to 110 degrees to keep their apparent wind forward, turning runs into something like another beat. Once again, watching the telltales and masthead fly will help you keep the apparent wind at about 120 degrees and pick out the lifts to jibe on.

THE UNDERLYING PRINCIPLES of light air tactics are that you have much less maneuverability, it takes a lot longer to get from here to there, wind shadows are more deadly, and saving momentum and speed is critical. Therefore, you have to look much further ahead into the future to plan you moves and escapes.

Around the starting line the congestion of boats makes the wind lighter and more disturbed. Avoid sailing below the line if possible. Stay out at one end or the other, where there's more wind and where you can get better wind direction readings. If you do want to get to the opposite end, do it to windward of the boats, not to leeward. Also, remember that broad-reaching is much slower than sailing close-hauled. It's easy to go upwind to check your sails and the wind, etc., and to get too far upwind of the line. Coming down is very slow.

Your final approach to the line begins much sooner in light air. I strongly recommend reaching in to the start on starboard, as opposed to tacking into a hole in the last thirty seconds and coming to a full stop. Timed runs are excellent, though you have to keep an eye open for wind velocity changes. Pick the spot on the line you'd like to start at and go beam-reaching past it on port with about four minutes to go. At two-fifteen to go, tack around smoothly. You'll be at your spot and going full speed after reaching for two full minutes. If you see you're going to be early, kill speed ahead of time so you can trim and be building speed in the last 30 to 45 seconds. Each boat is different and it's imperative that you know exactly how long it takes your boat to accelerate from stopped to full speed. Doing it a few times before the race will give you a good idea.

Try to avoid starting near a pack where you're forced to luff up and fight for position, because you usually won't have room to bear off to accelerate properly. This often means starting a ways from the favored end, but your full speed at the gun should quickly balance out the initial disadvantage. Also, a delayed start by about five to ten seconds at the weather end, followed immediately by a tack, is consistently a successful way to start.

Sailing upwind, look for clear air immediately. Try to minimize the amount you tack. If you aren't leading the race when you near the windward mark, consider overstanding a bit to be sure you have clear air all the way into the mark. In light air, boats bunch up at the marks more, and often you can gain a lot by going around the outside of all of them. Try to avoid coming in on port, especially if there is a long string of boats already on the reach.

On the reaches continually think in terms of the rhumb line. Only go above it if you absolutely have to. If you see boats ahead going high and you can work low, go for it. Your speed and momentum at the end of the leg will often pass you a pack of boats at the mark. However, the wind frequently comes in from above, so the bottom line is to keep your eyes open, standing up regularly to look for darker spots on the water, watching for flags and other boats sailing nearby (beware of cruising boats; it's amazing how high they can point with their engines on), and continually trying to sail as fast as possible

Probably the hardest thing about racing is light air is that, inside, your mind and body are going at full speed, but outside you have to sit absolutely still. The downfall of most people in light air – and I'm speaking from personal experience – is that they lose their concentration and their motivation to keep still, to adjust the sails constantly, and to keep looking ahead to see what the wind will do next. Recently I've resorted to a bag of granola and a cooler of ice water whenever I sense the blur of brain fade coming on. I can't guarantee what will work for you, but if you're like me and need some help keeping your mind fresh on those lovely light air days, anything's worth a try.

CHAPTER 9

Heavy Air Madness

From an interview with Paul Elvström:
Q: What's your favorite condition to race in?
A: (with a huge grin) A storm.

An Aussie's way of telling us it's windy:
"Why, it's blowin' the oysters off the rocks, mate!"
from the Book of Classic Foxallisms

HEAVY AIR: IT'S RAW PSYCHE, it's adrenalin, it's speed; it's tight-roping the jagged edge between hard racing and hurling through the water totally out of control. It's the sailor's Downhill. It's 470 sailors Eric and Richie Leitner wearing hockey helmets and knee pads to race, because "Man, it's war out there. Every tack you just got to put your head down and go crashing through the debris. I mean there's stuff flying around everywhere. It's like a jungle!"

But it's also the broken masts, the broken booms, the broken rudders; boats screaming down the reaches and just as suddenly self-destructing in explosions of water, only to emerge turtled. Finally it's the emotions. No one can hide them. You just don't see people rigging their boats with the same controlled look of confident anticipation for the upcoming race. Some are so hyper they can barely get into their wetsuits without ripping them apart. Others are so scared, they start to wear a trench between the toilets and their boat. And after it's all over it's the letdown, the release, the aches and pains and the total exhaustion that take over within seconds after the boat is put away. It's heavy air sailing, and through it all a few emerge who make it look easy.

Success and speed in heavy air grow from a combination of the following ingredients. First, you have to love it. Notice your mood when you wake up and the mailboxes are being blown sideways. If you suddenly want to mow the lawn, you might want to examine what it is you don't like about heavy air and then work on it. Second, you have to work extra hard to prepare your boat so nothing will break. Look over the boats of the best people in your class. Use line, wire shackles, blocks, and equipment that are almost too strong for the job. Check your hiking straps, especially where they're bolted or screwed in. Look for dry rot in your tiller, tiny cracks in your gudgeons and pintles, and small frays in your wire and line. If possible don't put any pop rivets or fittings near the tension wall of your mast or boom (front of mast, bottom of boom). The ugly fact is that for each hour of heavy air racing, you should plan on at least twice that much time to work on and prepare the boat.

Once you have all this under control, the only thing left is to go sailing. It's simple: the more you sail in heavy air, the better you'll get. Every class has its specific go-fast setting and techniques and its own masters of these. Before practicing bad habits, find the "masters" in your area and class, look at their boat, talk with them, and most important watch them sail in heavy air.

HERE ARE SOME THOUGHTS, observations, and techniques I apply to heavy air sailing. Upwind, use the jib to power the boat along, and use the main to keep the boat flat. The jib leads should come aft a bit to flatten the foot and open the leech. Keeping the headstay tight with rig and backstay tension will help flatten the jib. Moving the lead outboard will open the slot, which is often fast though it hurts pointing. In big waves or puffs when the boat becomes difficult to steer, easing the jib slightly will reduce the load on the helm. Otherwise, keeping the jib sheet pretty tight is fast.

The overall shape of the main should be pretty flat with an open leech. Tightening the outhaul flattens the lower sections and opens up the lower batten. Pulling the downhaul hard pulls the draft forward and opens the upper leech. Inducing lower mastbend flattens the forward section of the main, which widens the distance between the back of the main and the jib. The large wrinkles caused by this technique are okay, and are often called speed wrinkles. The result is a wider slot without having to move the jib leads outboard.

Pulling on the backstay will flatten the upper portions of the main and open the upper leech. Too much backstay can invert the jib with too much headstay load and can invert the main with too much mastbend. Be careful not to overdo it.

The vang in most classes should be set very tight, so that, if possible, the boom will not rise when the sheet is released. This is fast in boats from J/24s to 470s to Optimists. The helmsman then puts the boat on the fastest course based on the jib, gets everyone hiked out to the max, and plays the mainsheet constantly to balance the boat. As a puff hits or the boat begins to heel, ease the mainsheet as much as needed to keep the boat flat, and head up slightly. Once the boat is flat, hike hard, drive off slightly and trim in hard. As the forces on the board or keel, rudder, and sails begin to build up again, ease the main to release them. There may be times when half the main is luffing. Don't worry about keeping the main filled. Use the main to keep the boat flat, and keep the boat driving on the jib. Many top racers, including Soling and J/24 world champion Mark Bethwaite, Fireball world champ Joan Ellis and Tornado world champ Randy Smyth, have their crews play the main.

The worst thing in heavy air is to lose your speed. Crashing into a wave or letting your boat heel over is the quickest way into the parking lot. Steering is critical, as is your ability to concentrate for up to an hour or more at a time. Salt water in the eyes is very distracting, so when I sense a wave will spray me, either I raise my forward arm to protect my face or just "bat" the water away

in the air as it comes at me. I've never found that goggles or glasses help; however, a bike racer's squeeze container filled with fresh water to rinse my eyes out periodically is very helpful.

As I approach a wave that could slow me down, I try to see what's behind it. Just as top skiers look two or three moguls ahead, the same applies to waves. If I'm approaching a set of three or four, I'll bear off slightly to keep my speed and momentum. This means simultaneously easing the main to keep the boat flat and easing the jib slightly to keep the boat driving. (All through here is the shaky assumption that we're all perfectly straight-leg hiking and that all our muscles are functioning awesomely.) If the wave is followed by a flatter zone of water, I'll ease the main as the wave hits, and then quickly sheet in and squeeze up to weather a tad.

It's very possible that one strong reason for tacking will be to rest your mainsheet or tiller arm. But for whatever reason you decide to tack, remember you can lose big with a bad one. First, always be going full speed just before you tack. Never tack when the boat is heeled even slightly. Always look to weather so you tack into a smooth field, not a mountain range. Be sure everyone is ready (it's not a bad idea to have everyone say "ready" or something before you go). Never tack before the jib and main are out of their cleats. During the tack everyone should cross the boat as quickly as possible. Hike out even if the sails aren't filled yet. It's always fastest to have the boat flat immediately, even if it means heeling to weather momentarily. When you turn, turn extra far (maybe five to ten degrees past close-hauled). Be sure to use the mainsheet to keep the boat flat. If you or your crew are slow to cross, or if you've turned extra far and the boat is heeling, let out the main as much as necessary to bring it flat. Remember, flat is the key; don't worry if the main is luffing. The first 30 seconds after the tack are critical. The helmsman must be looking forward and steering well. Too many people finish their tacks looking at their crew trying to get their feet under the straps, or fooling with the mainsheets. (It's critical that your mainsheet arrangement can be easily cleated and uncleated from a hiked-out position.) Remember, a boat that is flat will accelerate faster and a boat that is going slowly is more susceptible to heeling or being blown into a capsize. Even before the start, always keep your boat flat and moving fast.

WHEN IT'S TIME TO GO DOWNWIND, you'll remember what you paid your money for! To me one of the greatest feelings is to be flying along and suddenly see the wave you're on drop off under your bow. With one quick pump, the boat simply launches into the hole and seems to double in speed. Jumping way back and trimming as fast as possible to keep up with the apparent windshift, you often find it impossible to see the bottom of the wave through the stream of water in your face, so keep your arm up as a shield. Just before you submarine into the back face of the Big Momma in front, cut up and head for the crest. While climbing, simultaneously ease out and hike so the centrifugal force of your turn doesn't heel the boat and bury your boom to leeward. Once at the top, hike hard, give a good solid pump on the sheet, and hang on as you take off on an even faster and longer ride.

While riding waves, remember to always keep the boat flat and continually play the sails. If the boat seems over powered, ease the vang. If your body drags in the water tighten your straps, cross your legs, or lean out sideways. Many boats have a tighter strap farther aft for the skipper downwind. As the boat accelerates, quickly trim all sails. Don't simply aim for the lowest section of each trough. Aim for the longest ride on the wave, and especially try to ride waves down below the rhumb line rather than up. Concentrate on using the speed of one ride to catapult you up and over the next wave. And most important: if you're trying to catch a wave but not succeeding, stop trying and wait for its little brother to catch up to you from astern.

The hairiest maneuver in heavy air is jibing. Dick Tillman once said, "As you're approaching the jibe mark in strong wind, remember one thing… never laugh at the guy ahead of you who just deathrolled!" The area around the Laser jibe mark is often known as the graveyard, not because people get hurt, but because when Lasers turtle, all the centerboards sticking up look like headstones. Remember the sage words on the Florida license plates, "Arrive Alive." If your get up and go already got up and went and you're feeling tired, don't take chances downwind. There's nothing wrong with tacking around at the jibe mark, but be sure to go at least five boatlengths past the mark before tacking. Also, jibing before a heavy air start is a devil's trap. Besides all the evils of capsizing, swamping, breaking your boom, or smashing your head, the planing before and after the jibe often takes you much farther away from the line than you might have planned.

If jibing is the hairiest maneuver, the hairiest ride in heavy air is dead downwind. The common accident dead downwind is the deathroll, or capsize to windward. If your rig is rocking and rolling a bit dangerously, put your board three quarters of the way down, overtrim your main, put more weight to leeward, move aft, and head up a bit. If you want to go faster, reverse all of the above. The best two sailors I've ever seen sail dead downwind in a breeze are John Bertrand and Cam Lewis (winners of two Laser Worlds and three Finn Gold Cups between them); without researching it, I'm willing to bet that the two of them had spent more hours and years in small boats going dead downwind in heavy air than anyone else sailing at that time. So whenever you get the chance, get out there and practice.

If you suddenly do get the urge to capsize, try to do it to leeward. Also, before the race be sure to tie everything into the boat, especially your scoop-bailer. If your boat has automatic Elvström-type bailers, be sure no lines can get near and clog them. "Catch" bags for tails and screens over the bailers both work well. It also helps to practice capsizing so when it happens in a race you can get up and going again as fast as possible. Finally, remember that you're going the fastest through the water the moment before you crash; so if you're capsizing a lot, at least you can tell people you were the fastest out there!

Racing in heavy air often seems like madness, but to most sailors it's our fix, our Dr. Feel Good, our champagne to the brain. It's the best feeling to know we're going to be challenged – by both the racing and the forces of the wind and the waves – and to feel our bodies slowly work up to a controlled frenzy before the race. Right then our muscles grab that extra ounce of strength, our nerve ends are electric, our senses become totally focused, and our inner timer starts ticking. We're alive, we're ready – and we love it. LET IT BLOW!

CHAPTER 10

Going for It Downwind: Speed

I HAD MY EYES OPENED to the game of downwind boatspeed when I started sailing Lasers in 1973. I had never sailed a high-performance planing boat till then, and I spent my first two years getting absolutely rolled. My downhill incompetence finally became glaringly evident to me at the 1974 Laser Atlantic Coasts. I had just rounded the jibe mark ahead of Pete Commette (1974 Laser world champ and unquestionably the fastest guy downhill at the time) and figured I'd better hold him high so he couldn't get past. But instead of going up he just said, "Forget it, Perry, you know I'm going to blow you off anyway." He bore off, took one wave through my lee, and by the time he rounded the leeward mark I literally couldn't read his numbers. Right then I decided I'd better get a handle on these downwind techniques. Now, after several years of carefully watching others, asking questions and experimenting, my downwind boatspeed is competitive, and I'd like to share some of the techniques that have worked for me.

The setup of the sails is straightforward – keep main and jib as full as possible, until overpowered. When the breeze is on, the outhaul and cunningham should be as tight as possible. (Tightening the cunningham hard is a good trick to suck out the main draft and spill open the leech without making the sail luff.) The vang should be played, keeping the upper leech just twisting open, until overpowered. Once overpowered let it all the way off to keep the boom from hitting the water, and the boat from rounding up.

The board should also be played continually, raising it as high as possible, until the boat starts sliding sideways (the helm will feel soft). I find that I generally have my board higher than most people I race with, but I also adjust it for major turns – down when I'm heading up for a big wave or for some tactical reason, and up after I've borne away. As soon as I'm broad reaching or running, I like the board close to its maximum up position.

As for body placement, the weight should be close together wherever it's located. In medium wind center the weight near the centerboard or keel; in light air move it slightly farther forward; and as the wind gets stronger move it progressively farther back (just enough to keep the bow from plowing). If the boat starts oscillating when dead downwind, spread the weight side to side to dampen the roll.

For fast sail trim, the leading sail is the most important. If it's a jib on a whisker pole, square the pole as much as possible without spilling too much wind on the leeward side. If it's a jib without a pole, do everything possible to enlarge the slot between the main and jib. It's usually best to have the crew sit on the leeward side, reach around the leeward shroud, grab the jib sheets and hold them away from the boat. At the same time the crew can apply downward tension to keep the upper leech from twisting off. If it's too windy for this, put on the barber hauler or quickly relead the sheet outside the shroud. The only way to optimize jib trim is with two telltales at eye level about a foot back from the jib luff. The windward telltale should be continually jumping around, but the leeward telltale should never jump, for this tells you the sail is stalled.

As far as main trim is concerned, the sheet should be held directly from the boom. Ease it till the luff just starts to bubble, trim a tad, then adjust it proportionally to every change in the jib trim. If the boat has only a main, you should have telltales on its luff and it should be continually trimmed like a jib.

As for trimming the spinnaker, this is a specialized art, requiring tremendous concentration and patience, plus a feel for shapes and subtle apparent wind changes. Here are a couple of key points: Whoever's on the chute has to be psyched to play the sheet and guy nonstop. The pole height is set by getting the luff to break in the middle, not by getting the two clews even. If the luff breaks high first, lower the pole, and if it breaks low, raise the pole. How far back the guy is trimmed is determined by how flat a chute you want. Heavier boats need fuller chutes, while planing hulls are faster with flat ones. On runs, even in heavier boats, I find it's faster to bring the guy farther back than most and trim hard on the sheet to flatten the chute and expose more area. The sheet should be continually played in and out so that the luff is curling over every three to five seconds. Curling the luff any less often is slow.

ONE OF THE BIG KEYS to downwind speed is anticipating apparent windshifts and reacting instantly. As the boat accelerates down a wave or in a puff, you know the apparent wind will shift forward and the sails will have to come in. The second the boats slows, runs out of the puff, hits a wave, etc., the sails must be eased in a big way. Leaving the sails overtrimmed is the quickest way to slow down.

As for steering fast dead downwind, the same principles apply as upwind, but in reverse. Sail too high and the boat goes faster but away from your destination, like footing upwind. Sail too low and the boat aims closer to the mark but goes slow, like pinching upwind. The game is to sail high and build speed, which increases the apparent wind and moves it forward. With the wind forward, coast down until the boat begins to slow, then head up and repeat the process. This scalloping course is the fastest way to sail dead downwind, especially in heavier boats. Lighter boats can get away with sailing closer to dead downwind, and for unstayed rigs, dead downwind and even by the lee a tad is fast, as long as the mainsheet can be eased enough to get the boom out perpendicular to centerline and beyond.

Once everything is set right, the real key to downwind speed is how you move the boat through the water, and a help with this is the direct feedback you get from the rudder. If you feel any tug, the rudder is stalled and your speed will suffer. When the boat is balanced perfectly, you should be able to relax your hold on the hiking stick and have the boat keep on going straight. (This is the reason why you should practice sailing without a rudder.) If the boat wants to head up, flatten the boat with crew weight, and if the crew is already flat out, then ease the main. It's always fastest to have the boat flat, even if you have to luff some of the main. If the boat wants to bear off, be sure your main is trimmed right and then lean in to leeward until the helm balances.

Every time you change your course, or anticipate that a puff or wave is going to change your course for you even the slightest amount, use your weight and sails to help reduce the drag on the rudder. If you're going to bear off down a wave, heel the boat to windward and ease the main a split second before moving the tiller, and do just the opposite for heading up.

Now, for planing in smooth water (no surfing), I try to anticipate the puffs so I'm the first one to jump up on a plane. This means continually looking around and watching for puffs on the water. The boat will accelerate fastest when it's flat and will be more stable the faster it goes. Also, remember that when the puff first hits, the apparent wind will jump well aft until the boat gets rolling again. So the game is to watch for the puff, then just as it hits hike hard and lean back to keep the rudder from rounding you up, ease the main as much as needed to keep the boat absolutely flat (a little pre-heel to windward just before the puff is really fast), bear off to get the boat moving, then quickly trim in the main as the boat accelerates.

Under rule 42, Propulsion, you are allowed one pump on each sheet to help get the boat planing. My experience is that pumping the jib is never fast, and that pumping the main is really fast if timed perfectly. The pump should come just as the boat begins to accelerate and should be as big and sharp as possible.

Once the boat starts planing, keep trimming the main more and more to the point of overtrimming for as long as the boat keeps accelerating and then quickly ease it. This is the one instance in which overtrimming is fast. The jib and spinnaker, however, should stay perfectly trimmed throughout – never overtrimmed. As the boat is planing you are creating a tremendous amount of breeze. If you sense the plane is ending, head up a bit to increase your speed and maintain the plane. If the sail luffs at any time, bear off instantly to fill it while you're trimming so that no speed is lost.

Sailing fast downwind is great, but to me the most fun is playing the waves, and this is where the biggest distances can be gained if you get hooked up and going. If there are waves, but not enough wind to surf them, then all they can do is slow you down. In these conditions I just try to find the path of least resistance through the water, and I usually wind up steering all over the place – heading up for speed and heeling in the chop and working back off again in the smooth sections. Even when you're not riding them, wave fields have high and low spots. The game is to bear off toward low spots and head up across high ones.

Now, when you're moving fast enough to ride the waves, there are a lot of techniques that are really quick. First, always watch your bow for the waves and remember that different waves are moving in different directions. Don't be tempted to ride waves away from where you're going, especially too high. As Commette says, "Watch for waves off your leeward bow, they're your bread and butter because you can surf them down toward the leeward mark or to leeward of the rhumb line and then head back up to pick up speed." When you're riding waves you have to study the water, always looking for a low spot to sail down into. Once you start surfing you'll begin to go faster than the waves, and you can use your extra speed to get up and over the humps and down the next one.

To begin surfing you have to increase your speed, just as a body surfer swims hard as the wave crests under him. If you see a wave building just up to weather, head up to increase your speed, sail up and over the crest and then ride down the slope. As you get near the bottom of a wave, be sure to avoid slamming into the backside of the one ahead. Either bear off farther and keep sliding down the face or use your speed to cut up across the one in front and down its face. This is a judgment call. If I see that I can ride down the waves and pick up another ride to leeward, I'll go for that. Otherwise I'll cut off early.

Sailing downwind takes a lot of concentration and energy to adjust your sails and weight continually while you're picking your way through the waves. But once you've got all the moves coordinated and you slip into the groove, things just get better and better, and you'll soon find you never want those downwind legs to end.

CHAPTER 11

Execution

"Using the rudder is a very inefficient way to turn a sailboat...
instead, use the body and sail, letting the rudder simply follow the boat.
– Carl Van Duyne, 1968 U.S. Olympic Finn Representative

SAILORS spend a great deal of parking lot and bar time talking about racing. Stick an ear into any of these conversations and you'll find that the majority of the topics relate to boatspeed. One guy is slow because he has a mast-tip weight that is 200 milligrams heavier than the rest. Or another is fast because his hull came out of a special mold that has since been destroyed.

All of these subjects are valid, but due to the talk time given them, they've grown wildly out of proportion with another boatspeed factor: simply sailing the boat up to its full speed potential all the way around the course. Of the equation *"Ability = Knowledge + Execution + Attitude,"* most sailors have more than enough knowledge about boatspeed and racing strategy, and in most cases attitudes are positive, but the execution – the actual sailing of the boat around the buoys – is the universal weakness. A good sailor who executes perfect roll tacks, eases his sails for every bad wave, and concentrates on sailing his boat at the optimum sail and weight trim level, all the way around the course, can more than overcome any inherent boatspeed efficiency, real or imagined.

To instantly discover if you're sailing your boat to its optimum level, go out in an uncrowded area in about eight-to-ten knots of wind, pull your centerboard halfway up, and remove your rudder and tiller. You should still be in perfect control of your boat, with the ability to head up, bear off, roll tack, roll jibe, and round marks. If not, it shows that, as you sail, you are constantly fighting forces on the boat, using your weight, the sails, and the rudder improperly. Practice is the only way to master this drill.

When practicing, don't just tie off the rudder – remove it. Try to practice with your regular crew, as it's important to learn to coordinate all movements in the boat. In using your weight to steer, heel the boat to leeward and it will head up. Heel the boat to weather and it will bear off. For sail adjustment, trim the main and ease the jib and the boat will head up; ease the main and trim the jib and the boat will bear off. Simple. At first, everything will happen very quickly, and the boat will probably spin in circles. But soon you'll note small changes making huge differences.

Try to reach the point where the sails are always trimmed optimally for the course you are on, and you are using only crew weight to steer the boat. Once you've achieved that, practice some roll tacks and roll jibes. Notice how the boat really reacts to your weight. Finally, practice the ultimate test of how well you've mastered the art of controlling the boat without the rudder – rounding marks. To test yourself under pressure, set up a short course and challenge your friends to a rudderless race, although you might want to check with your insurance agent first!

Once you've mastered rudderless sailing, put your rudder back on, but add a good, tight blindfold over your eyes. Most sailors rely too much on their sense of sight, leaving the other senses underutilized. With the blindfold on (and in an uncrowded area), sail upwind. With the skipper blindfolded, everyone in the boat suddenly gets involved. It requires that the crew actually start sailing the boat, making them realize how important it is to be looking around all the time, feeding the skipper clear and useful information about what's happening, such as "There's a puff coming in about 30 seconds," "Here comes a boat, better begin to bear away," or "You're sailing a touch light," etc.

The skipper should take a few long deep breaths and relax. Hold the hiking stick or tiller very lightly and feel the boat track through the water. Sense the wind on your face and the heel of the boat. If the boat begins to heel more, though the wind hasn't increased noticeably, you're probably bearing away too much.

While blindfolded, your ears should be your speedometer. Listen to the water as the hull moves through it, and try to sense when the boat speeds up or slows down. In the 1972 Olympic Trials, the Tempest team of Glen Foster and Peter Dean was always one of the fastest offwind. So after one particular race, when their speed on the first reach was noticeably off pace, Peter tried to put his finger on the reason. Finally, he realized that they had been followed down most of the reach by a photography boat. Apparently the sounds of the boat's engine drowned out the noise of their Tempest moving through the water. Dean then realized that, as he flew the chute, he determined the smallest changes in apparent wind by the sound of the hull moving through the water.

So, to strengthen your other senses, practice sailing blindfolded, experimenting with different angles of heel and different degrees of sail trim, trying to determine just what feels best. Finally, be sure everyone on board gets the opportunity to sail blindfolded. This will help them utilize all of their senses as well.

As you sail around the course, the wind, waves, and patterns of boats are always changing. Here are some techniques that will keep your boat going its fastest as you encounter those changes.

Responding to a Quick Lift

FIRST EASE THE SAILS to reattach the air flow, then head up. In a fast boat or a strong breeze, heading up might take place a split second after the sails are eased. In slower boats or light air, the time lag might be as long as five seconds. Crews must be alert to the telltales on the jib luff, easing the sail before the helmsman heads up. In lighter airs, quickly heel the boat slightly to leeward to help it head up.

Responding to a Quick Header

QUICKLY MOVE TO LEEWARD, as the boat will want to stand up or heel to windward. Momentarily add a touch of leeward heel, then, to help the boat keep up speed, return the boat to its optimal heel.

Responding to a Puff

KEEP THE BOAT FLAT. For every second you heel in a puff, you're going forward slower and sideways faster. Anticipate the puff and actually heel slightly to weather right before the puff hits. If the boat begins flat, it will accelerate quickly, the increased speed providing added stability. If the boat heels at the outset (when the puff first hits), it can be really difficult to bring back down. In puffy conditions, put your vang on fairly tight. Then, as the puff hits, sheet the main out as much as it takes to keep the boat level. However, always maintain optimum jib trim. It's more important to keep the boat flat and the jib full than to keep the main full. As you sheet out on the main simultaneously pinch up a tad and hike hard. Once the boat is zinging along, retrim the main.

Responding to Waves

CREWS SHOULD EASE THE JIB as the boat comes into a bad wave and retrim it afterward. Plan to play the sails continually as you sail through the waves. The skipper is the best judge of how much ease is correct, or feels right. Add a touch of heel as you approach a wave. Try not to hit the wave head on, but pick the path of least resistance. Generally this means heading up on the front of the wave and bearing off down the back. Study the water ahead to figure out what will work best.

Ducking a Boat

THIS IS A CRITICAL MANEUVER that many people take for granted, yet, done poorly, it can cost several unnecessary boatlengths. Cut a smooth arc through the water, never going beyond a close reaching angle and wind up close-hauled as you cross the other boat's transom. As you bear off, ease your sails, keeping optimum trim throughout by keeping an eye on the telltales. Also, as you bear off, be sure to keep the boat flat. When rounding up behind the other guy's transom, heel slightly to help cut across the wake and bad air, then bring the boat flat as you get back into clear air.

Roll Tacking

START YOUR tack with a slight heel to leeward, simultaneously pushing your tiller to leeward in a smooth arc. As the boat heads up into the wind, everyone on board should quickly move his or her weight to the old weather side, staying there until the boom crosses the centerline. Then, slowly bring the boat back to its optimal upwind trim.

Roll Jibing

IT IS ILLEGAL TO START THE JIBE with a slight heel to leeward. Simply roll the boat sharply to weather as the tiller is turned smoothly. As the boom comes flying across (in light air, someone should pull it hard by grabbing the vang or all of the mainsheet parts), the crew crosses the boat and resumes optimum downwind trim.

Sailing your boat properly around the course all the time is as important a part of boatspeed as having the right equipment; yet there is only one way to get it – practice. The next time you're out sailing to the line, impress your competition and do it without your rudder. When you get near the line, throw in ten quick roll tacks. Once the committee has set the starting line buoy, round it a dozen times, coming at it from different angles each time. Learning to sail your boat efficiently in five knots to 25 knots will be the most economical investment in boatspeed you can make, not to mention your increased improvement in finishing positions as you trim gobs of excess boatlengths off your trip around the buoys.

Tactics for Starting and Finishing

CHAPTER 12

Starting at the Weather End

IN WATCHING thousands of different starts, I've seen too many people hang back or put themselves in dangerous positions too often. Becoming a good starter obviously comes from experience, but it's the experience of getting in there, mixing it up and fighting for a front row seat that makes people better. This chapter is the first of a three-chapter look at starting.

There are two primary reasons why people hang back. First, they are unsure of the racing rules. This causes them to be overcautious and to stay away from the other boats, as they don't want to mess up their fellow sailors' starts. There are two excellent and quick ways to overcome this lack of knowledge. First, read *The Racing Rules of Sailing (RRS)*, and in particular the rules in Part 2 of the *RRS*. Preferably read them with a friend who really understands the rules. Supplement your reading with my text, *Understanding the Racing Rules of Sailing*.

Then enter a race as crew for someone who fully understands the rules. Have them point out rule situations as they occur, discussing the different rights and obligations as they change. Ask questions and get together after the race to refresh your memory. You'll find that the rules for any given situation are very understandable; it's the situations themselves that change rapidly. In a short time you'll be familiar with most of the situations as they happen and be able to apply the rules immediately.

The second reason why people hang back is the sense that their reflexes aren't fast enough to handle the close-quarters action. But most of us have driven down the highway at 60 mph (some of us may even have gone a touch faster). We've even handled lane changes and crowded stretches. What's more, we've done it in bad weather and at night, while listening to music, reading signs, and doing all sorts of other distracting things at the same time. In other words, your body is well prepared to handle events at 60 mph. Now, in an average 15-foot sailboat, 60 mph is about six boat-lengths per second, and unless you have a very quick boat, you don't ever have to deal with that kind of speed. In fact, your fifteen-foot boat is doing only about one boatlength every four seconds. So we all have the reflexes to get in there and mix it up.

LET'S THEN LOOK at the dynamics of starting at the weather end. When the line is square and no side of the course seems heavily favored, the fleet will spread itself out down the line. But in college racing, I started at the weather end more than 70 percent of the time. I prefer the weather end for several reasons. First, it is more forgiving. If I get a bad start I can tack and get into clean air and water sooner. Second, I can come in a little late with good speed, and tack immediately onto port. Even if I wind up directly astern of the first couple of guys onto port, I can drive off to leeward and quickly free my air. Third, it's extremely easy to judge exactly where the line is, as opposed to when I'm at the middle or even the leeward end. This assures that I'll be right on the line with full speed at the gun. Also I can hear clearly if my number is recalled, whereas the farther down the line you get, the harder it is to hear; and I'm right there at an end if I'm over at the one-minute rule.

The best approach to the weather end is from well outside the line. I call this approach "lurking in the shadows." Simply position yourself on starboard tack, five boatlengths to leeward of the extension of the line and with about one minute of full speed sailing required to reach the weather end (diagram). The key to starting at the weather end is knowing exactly where the layline is. The layline is the line on which a close-hauled boat would sail and just miss hitting the committee boat. Of course, even for the same class, the layline changes with different velocities of breeze, different boatspeeds and different sea conditions and current, so make several runs before the start to determine exactly where it is.

Once you are set up in position, which can be anywhere from two to one-and-a-half minutes to go, just watch as the others set up for their starts. If at about one-and-a-half minutes to go most of the fleet is on starboard and to leeward of the weather end layline, this immediately indicates that a) there will

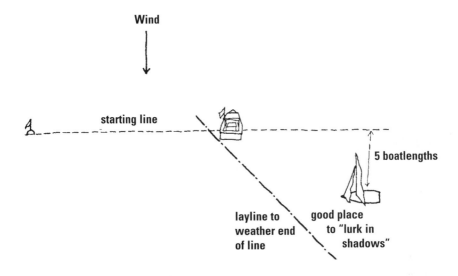

be little, if any, congestion at the weather end; and b) it may be heavily favored to start near the other end or go to the left immediately. From your vantage point, look down the line to see where the other good sailors are starting.

If you decide to stick with your strategy of starting at the weather end, simply get your boat wound up and plan to be close reaching, at full speed, past the stern of the committee boat with about two seconds to go. If you see one or two boats squeezing up to shut the door, you can safely assume that they will be falling off to a close-hauled course just before or at the gun. So just plan to arrive a few seconds late, and (with your full speed on) you'll either sail right over them, or at least be able to tack away into free air. This is a particularly good start for classes which accelerate slowly, such as keel boats in light air, and can be used very effectively, especially when the line favors the leeward end by as much as five degrees.

Now, if someone tries to challenge you for your weather end start, here's what to do. It all revolves around the layline to the weather starting mark. You're set up ready to come reaching in for the perfect start and another boat sets itself up in front of you. If you go to windward of them, they'll hold you up and force you on the wrong side of the starting mark. But what would happen if you started to sail to leeward of the boat? If they let you go through them, you will come up under them, become the leeward boat, and

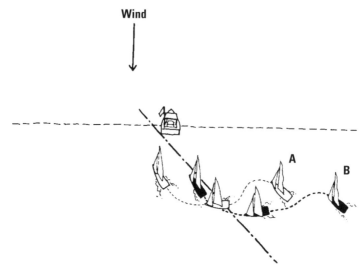

1) A challenges B for the weather-end start.

2) B bears off, as if to sail to leeward of A.

3) B waits until A has sailed beyond the layline to the weather end, then heads up close-hauled and takes the start.

force them above the weather end. So naturally they will bear off so as not to let you get to leeward of them. If they don't, simply sail behind them, give them room and opportunity to keep clear, then luff them above the mark. If they do bear off to defend against your intrusion on their leeward side, keep making it seem as if you are going to leeward of them, until they have sailed down past the layline to the mark (diagram). Once they're past the layline they can no longer physically shut you out. Then you can harden up to close-hauled on the layline and take the start. When tailing, be extremely careful not to overlap them to leeward unless you are 100 percent sure you can break through their bad air. If not, slow your boat down and stay on their transom. The key here is the layline, and you want to set yourself up so that, when you finally do get to the layline, you can head up to close-hauled and start without slowing down. In this way, anyone trying to duck your stern will not have enough time to break through your lee and will wind up in your bad air.

Sometimes you'll be lurking in the shadows, watching the fleet set up, and you'll notice that there's going to be a huge jam at the weather end. Remember a couple of things. First of all, packs of boats are moving slower and hence drifting downwind faster than single boats. Also, packs are very ingrown; sailors in packs are generally concerned only with each other. Finally, to leeward of most packs there's a rather large hole. So you can approach packs in a couple of different ways.

Watch the drift of the pack. Often the whole pack will be drifting downwind, especially if there's a lot of breeze or current, opening up a nice hole at the weather end. This will be magnified by the fact that the weather boats will be going very slowly and must fall off or go close-hauled at the gun. Even if you come swooping in five seconds late, you'll have speed and be able to prevent the weathermost boat from tacking onto port before you. But if it looks like a total jam, just reach in early and start to leeward of the pack. You really can't go wrong coming in from behind with speed, as there's usually a hole for you to get through. And if from your vantage point you see that the front row seats are filling up really quickly and there probably won't be any holes at the start, get on your horse early, get in there, and reserve a place for yourself.

The advantage of lurking in the shadow is that you let the other people set up first while keeping your options open to the very end. Therefore, the odds for getting a good start at the weather end are good, and it definitely helps avoid the aggravation and misery of getting a bad start farther down the line. Remember also that a five-degree leeward end favor (which a lot of committees do as standard practice) on a 500-foot line (average length for 25-to-30 15-foot boats), gives the boat at the extreme leeward end with the perfect start only a four boatlength jump over the boat at the weather end, most of which is equalized immediately after the start by the fact that the leeward end starter is probably not at full speed at the start, nor can he tack immediately to take advantage of a windshift.

CHAPTER 13

Starting at the Leeward End

"You pay your money, and take your chances, baby."
– Kojak

THAT'S THE WAY I look at trying to win the start at the leeward end.
Some people are famous for winning the leeward end whenever they want it.
But this is deceiving. Once people get a reputation for something like that,
others tend not to fight them as hard for it, making it easier for them to steal
the leeward end. More important, I've seen these same "famous" people get
eaten alive plenty of times, and even lose an important series because they've
tried to go for it.

Before we get into the dynamics of starting at the leeward end, remember that a good start is one that puts you in the front row, in clear air and

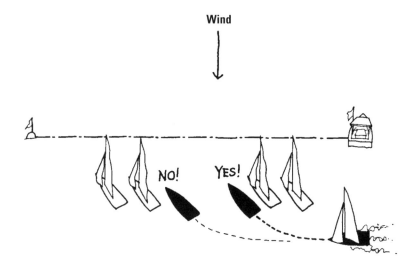

water, near the favored end of the line and going in the direction you want to go. Heed age-old, proverb number 226: "You do not need to win the start to win the race… and you do need to win the race to win the series." Unfortunately, many people give away races and series because they try to get too fancy on the line or just space out and completely blow the start.

EVERY BAD START is a result of violating one or more of the following six basic rules for getting a good start:

1. Don't get to the line too early and have to stop and wait for the gun.

2. Start close to full speed, regardless of where you start.

3. Start as close as possible to the boat to windward of you and as far to windward as possible of the boat to leeward of you (diagram).

4. Don't ever go in to leeward of a boat in final seconds before the start unless you are 100 percent sure you'll make it out into clear air on the other side.

5. If you feel like being conservative and hanging back at the start, do it only at the windward end.

6. Only try to win the start at the leeward end when you are 100 percent sure that you'll win it.

These guidelines are general, but they provide the basic formula for getting a good start and are well worth repeating to yourself each time you line up to start a race.

NOW LET'S LOOK at the techniques of getting a good leeward end start. First, you have to do your homework on the line. Especially when starting near the leeward end, it is imperative to have a good feel for a) where the line is, b) what the current is doing, and c) what phase the wind is in. Once the line has been set, see what its compass bearing is and get a good line sight. Both pieces of information are invaluable and much care should be taken to get them right. To get a line sight, position yourself just outside the starboard end of the line so that you can sight from one end to the other. Now look beyond the line to something on the shore that is easily identifiable – a tree or a tower, for instance. That is your Line Sight.

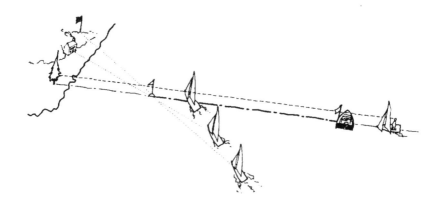

If you've never used a Line Sight, you should know that they are fantastic, and they can instantly turn you into a great starter, especially when starting at the leeward end. Quite simply, as you approach the line on starboard, look through the leeward pin toward the shore. As you draw closer to the starting line, your line sight will draw closer to your shore sight until, finally, the pin end and the shore sight will line up (diagram). You are now right on the starting line. Remember, of course, that you, personally, are on the line which means the bow of your boat is most likely over. Be sure to compensate for this! It is also imperative to know how much current, tidal and wind-blown, there is, and what direction it's moving in. The simplest way to determine this is to luff alongside the pin end of the line and look at the mark. Also note your drift. Armed with this knowledge you are ready to plan your approach. Surprisingly though, a large number of people who race rarely do their homework completely, either because they feel it's not important, or because they figure they'll probably get a bad start anyway.

Finally, to get a good start anywhere, you must know how quickly your boat will accelerate and slow down, and be able to accelerate it as quickly as possible from a standstill. If you've never practiced accelerating and slowing down, try it the next time you go out sailing. Repeat the exercise several times while experimenting with holding the boat at different angles to the wind, and using different tiller and mainsheet techniques. The best use of this drill is to do it side by side with a friend.

NOW LET'S LOOK at the different approaches to starting at the leeward end. Again, I'm not talking about winning the start, just getting a good start near the leeward end. The first set of approaches are the starboard tack approaches. Nothing to it really. Just come down the line on starboard and look around to see where you are in relation to the line. With one and a half minutes to go you should be about one minute of full-speed sailing from the leeward end and no closer than three boatlengths to the line. The heavier the air or the faster your boat accelerates, the farther to leeward of the line you should be.

Your goal is to be moving at the start, have your bow out in clear air, and have about one boatlength of clear water to leeward of you. As you move down the line on starboard, watch how the other boats are setting up. If there's going to be a crowd at the pin, stay upwind of the pack; if there are only a few boats down there, then slide down a little closer to the pin. Concentrate hard on keeping that one boatlength of open water below you. If you are successful at creating a "hole" below you, you can be sure of one thing—someone else is going to try to fill it. This is where the fun begins.

The attack will come from one of two places: either from behind and to leeward, or from a boat coming in on port. Here's how to defend against the port tack approach: As the port tacker approaches, simply bear off sharply and aim right at him. To avoid breaking rule 16.1, Changing Course, be sure not to change course in such a way that you prevent him from being able to keep clear. At this point the port tacker will probably pass you and look for a slightly more mellow person to start next to. As soon as the port tacker is by, luff back up sharply, using your momentum to try to regain the distance you just lost to leeward by bearing off. In a keel boat you can actually coast almost head to wind to climb back to weather.

If the port tacker does tack to leeward of you, quickly make a decision. Either he's far enough to leeward so that you can luff sharply and still have enough clear water between you, or he's closer than that, in which case you must quickly bear off, take his transom and come up to leeward of him on the other side. Note that if you do not bear off toward him immediately he will finish his tack securely to leeward of you, making it impossible for you to duck him.

Compared to the approaching port tacker, the starboard tacker behind you offers a threat more difficult to counter. To prevent him from ducking your stern and coming in to leeward of you, set up as far away from the line as you dare. This makes your stern less inviting because the ducker there would have to go too far to get around you. To further discourage duckers, simply bear off as you see one coming. Most boats will usually respond with a luff keeping them to windward of you. (To avoid losing extra distance to leeward when you bear off, overtrim your mainsail and turn sharply.) By staying low initially and bearing off each time a starboard tacker threatens to take your stern, you can effectively corral the fleet in the area to weather of you. You are now in position for your final approach (last 30 seconds) to the start.

The port tack approach is another way to get into a good position for your final approach. It is very effective when there is a lot of space on the line, i.e., small fleets, extra long lines, or a fleet in which the sailors cover a wide range of ability. It is also effective in boats that tack and accelerate very quickly, such as small planing-hulled dinghies and light centerboard boats.

THE KEY TO THE SUCCESS of a port tack approach is that you hang back, let the others do your dirty work for you, such as creating a nice hole in the line, and then swoop in at the last minute and fill it. This works particularly well for leeward end starts. Plan to be on port tack, well beyond the leeward end of the line, with about one and a half minutes to go and watch how the fleet is setting up. If there's going to be a big crowd at the leeward end, such as in large fleets of aggressive starters, get on your horse early and find a place before they're gone. Too often, port tack approachers wait too long, and by the time they get to where they want to tack, the fleet has set up two or three rows deep.

If there are many spaces, and you notice that the whole fleet is hanging back away from the pin, plan to come in at the last minute, tacking onto starboard into a nice hole and go. Often you can tack into leeward of the whole fleet and win the port end. The key to tacking in to leeward of boat on starboard is to do so as close to them as possible so that they are securely pinned to weather of you. Start your tack behind and to leeward of them so that the swing and momentum of your tack brings you alongside them. Also try to fin-

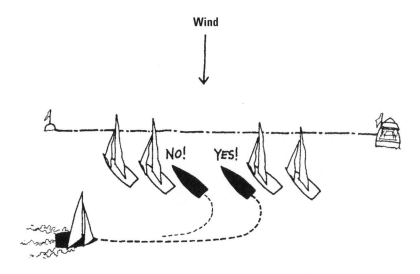

Wind

No!   Yes!

ish your tack as far away from the leeward boat as possible. (diagram). This is critical and is the place where many people make their mistakes.

Once you are in position, the final approach (last 30 seconds) is the most crucial. When the gun goes, you want to be moving at close to full speed accelerating sometime during the last 30 seconds. If you're already near the lines it makes it harder to accelerate without being too early. This is why it's important to a) know exactly where the line is, via your line sight; b) have a little space to leeward of you to reach off in and build speed; and c) be as far behind the line as you dare.

What generally happens is that too many boats try to start at the leeward end, causing huge jam-ups and a lot of chaos. It's best to avoid the whole mess, but if you do get caught in one of these jams, work like a madman to keep your bow slightly ahead of the guy to weather of you, snuggle yourself right up next to him, and start accelerating at least two or three seconds before he does – and you should come blasting out of there looking like a winner!

CHAPTER 14

Starting in the Middle

"Though my boatspeed wasn't as good as that of the rest of the fleet, there was one consolation (or so I thought) that made the 1975 470 Midwinters worthwhile: in every start, one of the top sailors would line up right next to me, and though they'd blow me off speedwise right after the start, I felt psyched that I was lining up in the right place each time. Unfortunately, after that year I heard a talk on starting by one of the guys who had repeatedly started near me. He said, "One of the most important things is to find a marshmallow – you know, some guy who is really slow – and line up next to him. All of a sudden, I realized that I was the marshmallow."'

– excerpt from a talk by a 1980 Olympic candidate

AN INCREASING TREND in starting is that the good sailors are starting more toward the middle of the line, which is not surprising since it offers them a lot of advantages. First, it gets them out of the congestion at the ends. Second, as in the above example, it gives them more flexibility as to whom they start next to (marshmallows beware!). And third, mid-line sag is a highly predictable phenomenon, meaning they can usually start safely, one half boat-length ahead of neighboring boats, which is all a good sailor needs to go blasting ahead of the boats which win the start at the favored end and they are in a good position to play any shifts and sail a conservative, smart beat up the middle of the course.

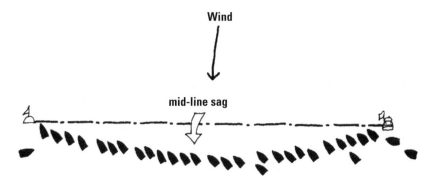

As the fleet becomes more aggressive, each sailor has to fight harder for position on the line and, typically, there is more bloodshed near the ends. As in politics and other more esoteric areas, the middle, besides having the advantage already mentioned, is simply the safest place to be. Before attempting a mid-line start, you should be thoroughly familiar with a couple of basic techniques, along with a few new trends on the part of both competitors and race committees, that may affect your starting success. The first key is to know exactly where the line is. This is particularly difficult to judge when you're near the middle, and most tend to be conservative and hang back. The result is mid-line sag, and the longer the starting line, the deeper the sag. The best way to overcome the sag is to get a good line sight (see Chapter 13). With about one minute to go, use your line sight to see where you are in relation to the line. If your view of the leeward end never gets obscured, you'll be able to use your line sight right up to the firing of the starting gun. This is a great feeling – you'll probably end up two or three boatlengths ahead of the fleet. Even if you do lose sight of the leeward pin, you can use the one-minute sighting as reference, eyeballing the distance you've moved up since then.

If you can't get a line sight, a good reference is to watch the boats at either end. If you're not close to being in line with them, you're probably a victim of the sag. Also, when you want to sight the line by looking from one end to the other, be sure to swing your gaze to windward of the boat, not to leeward. Swinging it to leeward creates the illusion that you're closer to the line than you really are. Another method of getting a good line reference when you can't get a line sight is to point your finger at one end, then "draw" the starting line across

Don't swing gaze to leeward of boat...

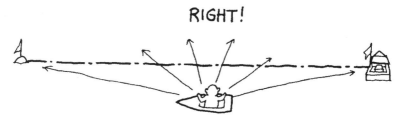

swing gaze to windward.

the water to windward of you and on to the other end. This means turning around in your boat so that instead of having your shoulders face to leeward, they're practically facing to windward. Then just keep an eye on the imaginary line you've drawn, and you should be in good position at the start.

Once you get comfortable knowing where the line is, you'll be able to start well in the middle every time. Just come in on port or starboard, set up as close to the windward boat and as far from the leeward boat as possible, and defend your position.

THERE'S NO QUESTION that quick acceleration is critical to start anywhere on the line, and there are several trends developing on this front, some legal and some not. One really sweet legal move that is particularly effective for planing-hull boats is to hang back, let a guy to leeward dig a nice, fat hole, and then come reaching across his transom and harden up right at the gun. By the time he knows what hit him, you'll be long gone.

Some illegal trends that are cropping up on the starting line involve rocking, pumping, and sculling. Again, this applies primarily to planing-hull or soft-chined dinghies. Rocking and pumping at the start not only quickly accelerate you, but can also effectively "walk" your boat to weather. These trends seriously hurt the nature of the racing, and every fleet should come down hard on people who clearly and intentionally violate the rules.

A much tougher question on people's minds today is, "If I know I'm near the line, and the people around me start going, do I go with them or hang back behind the line?" Unfortunately, the recent trend is to get away with what you can. The reasoning seems to be, "If I do hold back and start behind the line, even when others around me are flagrantly over, I'll have the moral satisfaction of knowing I wasn't over, but I'll also be completely nailed in the race. Everybody's doing it and getting away with it, so I guess it's now part of the game."

The roots of the problem parallel the roots of the social crime problem. For a system to work without the threat of external punishment, each member of the system has to respect the rules and play by them. As soon as one or two don't and start gaining an advantage, the rest are forced to either try self-policing, which in starting is almost impossible, or join in.

Once the masses have joined in, on comes the need for external punishment, which grows worse and worse until the problem is back under control. And believe me, race committees have an arsenal of weapons at their disposal. One choice is to arm each end of the line with an official boat empowered to call premature starters. This greatly reduces the overcrowding at the leeward end. Tactically, when the leeward end is an official boat, start up the line from it, because premature starters are very easy for them to spot.

The artillery of the race committee includes the one-minute "Round the Ends" rule (rule 30.1), which requires you to go around one end or the other if you are over once either rule goes into effect. One very helpful trend is for the race committee to hail the boats as soon as they violate the rule rather than waiting for the starting signal. When this rule is in effect, try to start closer to an end just in case you have to reround.

When there are several premature starters, many committees will call in their bigger guns – hailing as many boats as they can and letting the rest go. Though this system is unjust, it does have the effect of keeping people back near the ends and encouraging people to slide down the line toward the sag in the middle. Occasionally, however, people near the middle who feel securely hidden will start going early, causing a mid-line bulge instead. It's the old ostrich theory at work: "If I can't see them, then there's no way they can see me." In practice, it takes a damn good race committee to prove this theory wrong.

But the real weapons are the stricter one-minute 20% penalty and DSQ rules (rules 30.2 and 30.3). Here, if you are caught over in the final minute before the start, you're given a 20% penalty in that race or disqualified from that race. The strategy here used to be, if you're going to be over, drag half the fleet over with you to insure a general recall. But then the committees got tougher. Now, if you're over, you're out – disqualified for that start and all subsequent starts of that race. Though it sounds unfair, it works and so committees use it. Start safely and conservatively (i.e. well hidden) in the middle of the line and don't worry – the first ten boats that beat you will probably get penalized anyway.

One frightful trend which is growing more and more popular is identifying the handful of boats behind the line at the start, assigning all the rest as premature starters. In CORK '78, with a Laser fleet of over 80 boats, the fellow who crossed the finish line 53rd got the gun. Imagine his surprise! Of course, the real bummer is when the committee gets so frustrated with numerous general recalls that they give up, pull anchor, and head for home, but I suppose that's better than lowering the aim of the starting cannon.

With fleets of sailors becoming better and better, the demands on starting skills have grown tremendously, and without a good repertoire of starting tactics, you may as well save yourself the agony and stay at the club bar. The same repertoire of starting skills is required of race committees; much of the "social crime" that sailors are forced to partake in is caused by overly short or biased lines. The obligation to get off to a good clean start is the equal obligation of racer and race committee, and when there is confusion, delay, or a massive number of general recalls, knowledgeable representatives from both groups should get together and try to resolve the problem before the next day of racing.

The Great Escape

WELL, SO THAT PERFECT START didn't work out quite as well as you'd planned. No problem. Statistics show that every sailor gets a minimum of one, and sometimes even two, bad starts in a series, so you're right in there with the best of them.

Now you just have to figure out the best way to pick yourself up and get back in the race. With most bad starts, you know that you're going to have a rough one as early as 30 seconds to a minute before the gun. So don't feel you have to wait until the gun goes to make your escape from a bad start. Bail out as soon as you realize you're not going to make it up to the line or into clear air. The classic example of someone stubbornly refusing to bail out is the guy who is coming up from leeward with no real chance of breaking through boats already on the line. But instead of tacking out of there and looking for another hole, or at least getting off into clear air farther up the line, the guy continues, yelling "Up, up, up!' and swearing at his crew for not trimming the jib in soon enough. Finally, the gun goes, sealing his fate. The air is so bad, oxygen masks automatically start dropping from his boom. The water is wildly churned up, and the whole fleet has hardened up to close-hauled, preventing him from tacking and sealing all possible escape routes.

The key to avoiding this is to anticipate the trouble before it happens. One time I was sailing Lasers in about 18 knots, and I was luffing on the line with about 30 seconds to go. All of a sudden there was this incredible noise and yelling, and I looked back to see this guy planing madly down the line, totally out of control. I was so intrigued by the sight that I watched him zip by my transom and head for a hole below me. He then hardened up a bit too fast and instantly deathrolled to weather. Unfortunately, he had gone just far enough so that his mast came crashing down like toll-booth gate right on top of my bow. Then, BANG! The gun went off. Great! The only thing that would have saved me at that moment was a Black & Decker power saw. Had I been thinking clearly and anticipating the possibility of trouble, I could have bailed out before it happened and been off with the rest of the fleet.

If you're starting near the windward end, you may encounter several variations of bad starts. The first is getting to the line too early and being pushed over by the boats behind. Too often, a sailor who knows he's going to be early just sits there and waits for it all to happen. Maybe he thinks he can jam up the rest of the fleet to windward, forcing a general recall. (He can't believe that the committee will get his number. But sure enough, nine times out of ten, the committee will spot him.) If you know you're going to be over, bail out! Either bear off and try reaching into a hole farther down the line or, better yet, sail up around the committee boat and start again. If you do this at twenty seconds rather than waiting for the gun, you'll still be in the race. If you're caught coming into the weather end too low, simply tack and try again. Your chances of getting a good start are much better than if you stay down and try to break through from the rear. One thought on tacking back onto port – avoid jibing at all costs. You'll wind up much farther away from the line than you thought, as well as risking a capsize, particularly if it's breezy. It's better to bear off, tack and duck starboard tackers. Finally, if you know you're going to get boxed out at the windward end and get caught for barging, circle around and restart. If it's done early, you'll get a decent start. If you have to do it after the gun, you'll have a much worse start than necessary. Remember, no one can go anywhere before the gun has gone – so that is the time to do all of your circling and repositioning.

The same applies for starting at the leeward end. Too often, people know they're going to be early at the pin. But instead of jibing out of there and setting up again, they luff and pinch and squeeze and holler, ending up either hitting the pin anyway, not making the line at all or, the worst of all bummers, accidentally falling onto port tack. If you sense you're going to be early at the pin end, bail out of there, and do it soon! If you wait until the gun goes to make your escape, you'll end up getting a quick review of the name of each boat in the fleet as you pass behind their transoms.

In bailing out onto port tack, there's one rule that is frequently misunderstood, but that is vital to recovering from a bad start. Rule 18.2(a), Giving

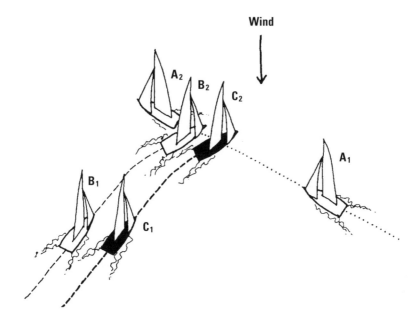

A is on starboard with B and C ducking her transom. C must give B room to pass astern of A.

Room; Keeping Clear requires an outside overlapped boat to give an inside overlapped boat room to pass an obstruction. A right-of-way boat can be an "obstruction" (see definition of Obstruction), and between two non-right-of-way boats the outside boat of the pair must give the inside boat room to pass the obstruction. This frequently occurs as two port tackers are passing the transom of a starboard tacker. If the outside (leeward) of the pair chooses to pass behind, they must give the inside (windward) boat room to do likewise (diagram). Of course, under rule 19.1, if the outside boat chooses to tack, they can do that also, provided they fulfill all obligations clearly stated in the rule (also see Appeal 36).

Now the gun has gone, and you're back in the bushes. Don't freak out – the race just becomes a bit more challenging, that's all. Remember, the fleet can't get too far away from you in the first minute or so after the start, so quick reactions can often get you right back into the action. The problem with a bad start is that most people think they have to shoot a corner to get back into the race, and they wind up losing even more. It's the old "well, let's see, most of the fleet is going left, so we'll bang it to the right" syndrome. But the race is long, and the series longer, and I can't count the number of times after the series is over that I've wished I'd fought it out for 15th place in a race rather than gambled and wound up 25th. Hang tough, and get what you can.

FIRST OF ALL, you should definitely have an idea as to which side of the course is favored. Also try to notice which way the top sailors are headed. Set your boat up for more power as you sail through the disturbed water and lighter air, i.e. fuller sail – eased outhaul, cunningham, and sheet tension. But be sure to shift back down when you get off into clear air again.

At this point, clear air is vital. After a start the first thing that will happen is that boats will begin peeling off onto port tack. The sooner you can do that, the better. Crews should be carefully watching traffic so that the skipper can concentrate on keeping up speed. If on starboard and another boat close to windward is preventing you from tacking, you can often tack and clear that boat's transom by bearing off sharply or by quickly luffing the mainsail, rather than waiting for them to tack. Once on port, someone onboard – preferably the crew – had better keep eyes wide open. As a general rule, it's better to duck a starboard tacker and continue on port into clear air than it is to tack on their lee-bow. Only lee-bow a boat if you want to go to the left very badly, you'll be in clear air on starboard, or you'd have to duck a lot of boats before hardening up again. Often, in a close situation, a starboard tacker would rather have you cross their bow than to tack on them. Always ask, "Tack or cross?" and watch for their response. The alternative to tacking is to drive off to leeward of the boats ahead, putting you in clear air. Remember, a boat or pack of boats throws bad air off in a cone-like pattern. Also the bad air is worst when you're closest to the boats ahead. When in a boat's wind shadow, most people feel themselves start slipping back pretty fast, and tack or bear off at that point. But after two or three lengths, you really don't get hurt that badly. So, if they're going the right way and you're not getting seriously hurt, hang in there.

One advantage to getting a bad start is that you can see what's happening to the boats ahead. The first few boats to get a header will not always tack immediately, for they want to be sure the header is real. You can watch them, and if the header is sticking, tack as soon as it hits you. You'll have a slight jump on the boats ahead and a bigger jump on those who are sailing out of phase with the windshifts.

Another good tactic for fighting your way out of the jungle is what Gary Jobson calls "the starboard-tack blocker." If you want to tack to starboard, first duck a starboard tacker and tack to weather and behind that boat. That sets the other boat up as your "blocker." Then, as port tackers come across, they'll first encounter your blocker, located to leeward and ahead of you. If they can't cross, and decide to tack on the blocker's lee-bow, it will hurt the blocker, yet you'll remain in clear air. If they decide to duck the blocker they'll probably have to duck you as well. You'll be pleasantly surprised, the first time you use it, how effective this tactic is.

Fighting your way back into the race after a bad start is one of the toughest skills in sailing. It requires that you keep your eyes wide open, anticipate openings into clear air even before they happen and know exactly how your boat handles. Most important, it requires that you keep your cool throughout the entire race. Being back in the pack is no fun, but if you keep your head together and never stop fighting, you probably won't be there for long.

CHAPTER 16

Everything You Always Wanted to Know about Finishing Upwind

IF YOU'RE PROFICIENT at the Buddy Melges style of racing – start first, pull away at the first mark and extend your lead – you probably have no problem figuring out what to do when you get to the finish line. But most of us find ourselves approaching the line with boats pouring in all around. In that case, you have to do some extra thinking.

If the sailing instructions aren't clear as to what the two ends of the line are or where the line will be located, be sure to ask. Next, think about what the wind is doing. If the wind has been oscillating every five minutes and you're about four minutes from the line, you know that you'll have only one more shift before you finish. In other words, treat the last shift into the line as a persistent shift because it won't shift back before your race ends. It's especially important to get to the inside of a group of boats if you're going to get lifted, which means you may have to eat a header and pass behind some boats to get there.

You should also look ahead at the finish line flags to find out what the wind is doing at the finish. They'll tell you exactly what is happening with the wind up there and what kind of shift is moving down toward you. Also, notice how the boats ahead of you are finishing because even though they've hammered you in the race, their sailing angles and tactics can still give you a better idea of how to sail to the finish.

As soon as you're close enough, scout out the finishing area. At the Laser Worlds in Kingston, every boat turned right toward the harbor after finishing. When about 40 of the 100 boats had finished, there was quite a parade

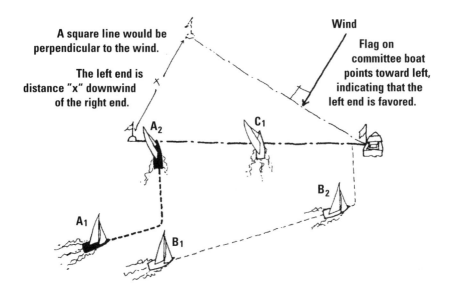

A square line would be perpendicular to the wind.

The left end is distance "x" downwind of the right end.

Wind

Flag on committee boat points toward left, indicating that the left end is favored.

C finishes perpendicular to the line, indicating that the left end is favored. A notes C's finishing angle and the line position relative to the wind and finishes at the left end. B, on the other hand, finishes at the right end, losing out in the process.

headed down the right side of the course, completely blocking the wind there. Particularly when you're back in the pack, it's important to stay clear of this kind of disturbance whenever possible. You should also be aware of bad air from the spectator and race committee boats.

Now that you have the line figured out, decide which end, if either, is favored. Simply put, determining the favored end of a finish line is just a matter of deciding which end is farther downwind. To do this accurately, there are several tricks. First, avoid the optical illusion that the larger end is closer. With a committee boat and a mark, the boat always seems to be closer until you get there. Also, you can't always tell the angle of the line to the wind by the way a committee boat is hanging on its anchor, especially if there's any current. However, flags are usually reliable wind indicators, particularly if they're set high up on the boat or near the bow. If the flag on the right end of the line is almost pointing at the left end, then the left end is much farther downwind and therefore favored (see diagram).

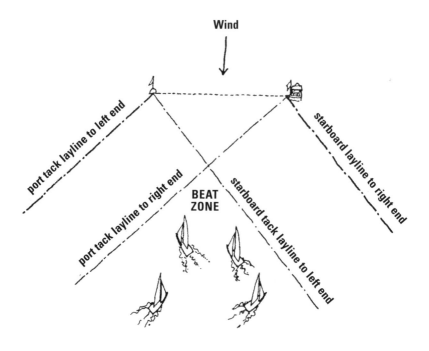

Another indicator of the finish line angle is the boats that have already finished. If the line is square, those boats should be cutting the line at roughly a 45-degree angle. If you see a boat finishing on starboard and they're perpendicular to the line, you know that the left end is farther downwind and again favored (see diagram).

Often the race committee will run a course with the start and finish in the middle of the beat so they don't have to reset the line. If the wind and the line haven't changed, then the end opposite the one favored at the start will be favored at the finish.

A general rule which always applies is: finish at an end of the line, never in the middle. In the middle, it's harder to judge when to shoot the line. It's also more difficult for the committee to see and read your number if you finish in a crowd. And, if the line isn't perfectly square, you'll be sailing extra distance. Combining this rule with the importance of finishing at the favored end, all of your tactics for finishing revolve around knowing where the laylines for the finish lines are. The laylines are determined by the close-hauled course you would sail to take you straight to one end of the line. Each mark has two laylines, and in determining them, remember that they'll be affected by any current in the area and by windshifts (see diagram).

Having located the laylines, there are several tactical ways to use them. In general, as you're approaching the line and trying to decide which end is favored, stay in the "beat zone" (downwind of the two inside laylines) for as long a possible. This keeps your options open. Once you've determined which end is favored, go all the way to that end's outside layline and come in with full speed right at the mark. Now, let's discuss a few specific situations.

- If you're approaching the line on port, but plan to finish on starboard at the favored left end, be sure to tack to starboard right on the left end's inside layline. This way, if a boat lee-bows you, they'll have trouble making the mark, and if they duck you, you'll beat them across the line.

- If you're the boat coming in on port and you find a starboard tacker near the inside layline of the left end, you have two choices. If they are right on the layline or have slightly overstood, you can tack on their lee-bow, which leaves you in a position to start shooting the line first or to actually cross the line first, assuming you can fetch the end. Remember that if you tack within two-lengths of the mark, you cannot thereafter cause the starboard tacker to sail above a close-hauled course to avoid hitting you (rule 18.3, Tacking at a Mark).

  If you don't think they'll make the mark, then duck with full speed and tack the second you're on the layline. Then, when they tack, assuming they can't cross you, they'll be in a pickle and forced to either duck you or attempt to squeeze in a lee-bow at the mark. Remember, they have to complete their tack by falling off to their close-hauled course (rule 13, While Tacking) and then give you room to keep clear (rule 15, Acquiring Right of Way) before they can shoot head-to-wind at the mark. Plus, if they tack within two-lengths of the mark, they cannot shoot up to the line if it causes you to sail above close-hauled to avoid hitting them. You can really make life tough for them by bearing off to where you'll have to shoot head-to-wind to make it yourself, but be sure to do this before they are so close that they'll immediately have to change course to avoid you (rule 16.2).

- If you're on starboard, just shy of the left end inside layline and a port tacker ducks you, tack as soon as it crosses your transom. You will have pinned it and should be able to push it past the inside layline, at which point you tack for the mark. Of course, if you hesitate and the other guy is sharp, he'll tack to starboard as soon as you tack to port, and if both boats hit while tacking, you'll be out (rule 13).

- If you're in the same position and a port tacker tacks on your lee-bow, be sure to push it well past the outside layline before tacking. This tactic breaks no rule. You are simply preventing the boat from tacking onto port due to your proximity. When you do tack, be sure it is not overlapped on your inside; otherwise, the boat is entitled to room (rule 18.2(a)).

- If you find yourself pinned on the outside of the left end by a windward starboard tacker, try to force an early tack by the windward boat, either by a few sharp luffs or a little friendly verbal persuasion. Then, as soon as the windward boat goes, tack immediately. If you're overlapped, you're entitled to room. Of course, if the outside boat is good, it will give you just enough room, but still swing its bow up across the line before you.

- If the right end is favored and you want to finish on port tack, be sure to overstand the right end's inside layline by about a boatlength, so if you have to duck a starboard tacker, you'll still be able to make the line without tacking. If you're coming in on starboard near the outside layline of the end and there is a big committee boat at that end, pass a couple of lengths to leeward of it to avoid its wind shadow.

AT SOME POINT in all finishes there comes the time to shoot the line, and there are two important rules for shooting: always shoot at full speed, and always finish perpendicular to that line. If you always finish near an end, it's easy to know when to shoot. It also helps to try to watch the eyes of the committee member sighting the line to know exactly where the line is. By finishing perpendicular to the line, you are sailing the geometrically shortest route to the line. The trade-off is, of course, that you lose speed when luffing.

So, plan your shoot to last no longer than a few seconds. In good shooting conditions, such as in smooth water, aboard a heavy boat, or in a favorable current, shoot sooner. In chop, light air or with an opposing current, wait until the last possible second.

One other tip about close finishes: note whom you finished ahead of and behind. Sometimes the committee won't get everyone, and you can save yourself from a DNF or lower position by noticing who finished around you.

Now, a quick review of some of the rules at the finish. First, if you're ever confused as to which way to cross a finish line, the definition of finishing clearly states that you cross the line from the direction of the course from the last mark.

Coming into the finish line, the ends of the line are marks of the course and are treated like any other marks (except starting marks surrounded by navigable waters) with regard to buoy room. If an inside boat has an overlap when two boat-lengths from the mark, the outside boat must give it room (rule 18.2(a)).

By the definition of finishing, you've finished when any part of your hull, crew, or equipment in its normal position crosses the finish line. Once you have crossed the line, you can clear the line in either direction (rule 28.1, Sailing the Course). If there's a strong current against you, just stick your nose over the line, then back away and you're all set. Of course, under the definition of racing, you're still subject to the rules until you've cleared the finish line and finishing marks. Clearing the line means that the finish line does not pass through any part of your boat (Appeal 16). Clearing the finishing marks means that if you try to sneak in along a committee boat with the flag in the stern and get your transom clear of the line, but then hit the boat, you're still racing and you must take your penalty and cross the line again (Appeal 26). The only time you can be DSQ'd after finishing is for interfering with a boat that is still racing (rule 22.1, Interfering with Another Boat; Appeal 16), so be careful as you clear the finishing area.

Let's hope you'll always be way out front and all alone when you finish, so you won't have to worry about all this stuff. But when you do find yourself coming in with company, it's a good feeling to "out-tacticalize" them right on the line and come out on top.

Tactics for Racing Upwind and Downwind

CHAPTER 17

From the Inside Looking Out

ONE THING that has always fascinated me is to hear what other people actually think about and say on their boats during a race. We've all heard the stories in the parking lot after the race, full of 20/20 hindsight and creative interpretation. Even articles and books written in the first person are still one or two steps removed from what was actually encountered on the course. I suppose the best way would be to secretly plant a tape recorder on board an excellent sailor's boat. But that borders on the unethical. So, we're left with very few alternatives, one of which is reporting the thoughts and conversations that go on aboard our own boat during a race. That's what I'll try to do here.

THE RACE I've chosen was the third race of a Soling Nationals, sailed on Biscayne Bay. It was a pretty interesting race in which we managed to finish fourth, and as I was already thinking about writing this book, I sat down and recorded our dialogue and the thought processes involved immediately after the race.

I sailed with two friends, Peter Isler and Tucker Edmundson. As helmsman, Peter's main job was to drive the Soling around the course as fast as possible. Upwind, he worked in conjunction with Tucker, who was continually adjusting jib trim. Offwind, Tucker flew the chute. My main concern, upwind and down, was noting our position relative to other boats and making tactical decisions.

The second and third races of the series were being sailed back to back, and we had just had a miserable morning race. So, while eating our lunch and sailing back down to the line for the afternoon race, we tried to pinpoint what went wrong. Among other things our start wasn't especially stellar, and we decided that we had wandered down the line too far on starboard before turning back for our port tack approach. As we planned to start up near the weather end this lured us into staying on port too long before going back onto starboard for our start. As a result, we never did make it into clear air in the front row, and were forced to bail out shortly after the gun, never really making it back into the race.

Then we discussed which side seemed favored and what the wind was doing. It was an incredibly shifty breeze, with huge puffs and lulls. It seemed about 75 percent of the puffs came in from the right and were big starboard tack lifts. But then again, there were definitely a few big port tack shots from the left. One thing seemed certain – the middle was a bad place to be.

We finished repacking the chutes, got the boat completely set up for the next race, and headed directly for the starting line area. Once there we took a wind shot to see what direction the wind was from at that particular moment – 050 degrees, as far right as we had seen it during the morning race.

The breeze was also a bit stronger, and we considered changing to our heavier air sails, but a quick look up the course at the other boats sailing upwind showed us enough holes to make us decide to stay with the light air sails. We then went upwind on starboard to get all of our controls set for the next race and discussed what changes we'd instantly make as we encountered the puffs and lulls. We also noticed boats up the course sailing at about our same angle, but on the opposite tack. So we knew we were in for another wild one!

BY NOW the starting line was set, and the compass course to the first mark posted – 035 degrees, same as in the last race. Peter swung us outside the weather end and aimed us right at the leeward end. With the two ends lined up, Tucker read the compass heading while I noticed the line sight – a white roof just to the left of a rise in the land. The compass bearing of the line was 305 degrees, perpendicular to the posted compass course to the first mark. We shot the wind again and found 040 degrees. This favored the right-hand end by five degrees, meaning the wind was still in a right phase, but moving left. We had seen the breeze as far left as 025 degrees in the first race, but not very often.

The ten-minute gun had already gone, and we figured that the bulk of the fleet would be at the right-hand end, due to its slight favor at the moment and the fact that the right side of the course had generally paid in the first race.

I stood up to get a better look at the conditions to weather. The water looked pretty patchy. Puffs were rolling in, and they seemed to last anywhere from 30 seconds to three minutes, so it was difficult to tell what was going to happen next. We shot the wind again and found 035 degrees – meaning the line was now square and the wind moving left.

"3:45 to go, Pete."

"Okay," Pete replied. "Let's back down for a second." (The northerly breeze had blown a lot of weed onto the bay that week.)

"Let's try and start to leeward of the pack, about one-third of the way down the line, and head left for a while," I suggested. At about two minutes, we were on port tack headed up the line and looking for a hole. "Hey, seems like the breeze has gone even farther left," I said. "Let's slide down a little closer to that end." We flipped onto starboard, got the boat moving up to full speed at ten seconds and crossed the line with about five boats (out of 43) to leeward of us. "Okay, Pete, speed's good. We have a guy to leeward, so don't drive too much. We can't tack right now."

After about a minute we got even more of a knock, and the boat to weather of us tacked off on a nice crossing slant. "Okay," I said, "pick your place and go." As one bad wave during a tack will completely stop a Soling, I tried to give Pete some warning so he could pick a flat spot. We ended up tacking about two lengths later, which was plenty to keep us out of the bad wake and bad air of the boat which had tacked just prior to us. Unfortunately, the left shift didn't last as long as we had expected, and soon the boat to leeward and ahead – Bill Allen – was forced to tack back by a starboard tacker – Dave Curtis.

As the breeze was now going right, and we'd have to duck a lot of boats to stay on port in clear air, I chose to stay to leeward of the pack in anticipation of the next shift. We tacked in to leeward of Allen, but not in a position to immediately hurt him. Unfortunately for Allen though, the shift had come with a big blast, and while Curtis, with 410 pounds of crew weight over the side, had already shifted into the driving mode, we were set up to pinch to keep the boat flat. Soon Allen got the squeeze play from Curtis and us, and he was forced to tack away. The new situation quickly became apparent: "Curtis will roll us before we can get up and pinch him off," I said, "and we want to keep going left, at least for now." Instinctively, Pete dropped both the main and jib traveler cars to leeward, and we began to foot with Curtis, breaking almost even speedwise.

After about three minutes of silent sailing on starboard the wind began going left again, and the two or three boats to leeward started looking better and better. I told Pete to put it back on the wind again, meaning that, due to the header, Curtis was no longer in a position to roll us, and we could pull the traveler cars back up again. Soon we were down 15 degrees, Curtis tacked off, and we tacked about four boatlengths later. Now for the big trek across the fleet, praying that the lift will last until we get to the other side.

AT THIS POINT, things were silent except for an occasional "Ease" from Pete when he wanted Tucker to slack the jib for a bad wave or a light spot, or "Heel" when he felt the boat getting too upright. In the lulls, Tucker automatically eased the jib a touch. At the same time, Pete eased the backstay and mainsheet, opening up the leech, making the mainsail fuller and sagging the headstay, which made the jib fuller. I eased the boom vang and main cunningham to keep the lower portion of the main full. As the breeze came back on these changes were reversed, and all of this happened with no conversation. We were all concentrating hard on what we were doing.

Now we were not far to leeward of the port tack layline, perhaps one minute's sail on starboard tack, but we had close to ten minutes of sailing on port to get across to the starboard layline, and a lot can happen in ten minutes! There were two boats up inside of us, which we could cross by five lengths if we tacked. Curtis was off to leeward and footing away from us slightly. He could cross us by one length if he tacked. The rest of the fleet was well down to leeward and slightly ahead, and though none could touch us at this point, with a header we could be as deep as tenth place. Pete and Tucker were both into their jobs, and since they could also see what was happening, I just reported on our boatspeed: "We're climbing out a little on Curtis, but he's footing a tad faster. He's gained a bit on us. We're coming up nicely on the boats to weather and seem to have even speed with the boats to leeward."

By now, we were within two minutes of the starboard tack layline, and the wind was going back to the right. Curtis tacked and crossed us by five lengths. Two other starboard tackers were coming, and it was going to be close. I decided that the wind was definitely continuing to shift to the right and would probably continue until we rounded the weather mark, about three minutes away, as the wind had been left for so long. So I said, "Pete, duck the red boat on starboard." By ducking, that second starboard tack boat crossed us by two lengths. It was Allen again. I looked to leeward and saw an even bigger starboard lift on the boats there, so I called for a tack just shy of the starboard layline, to leeward and ahead of two other boats – Jim Coggan and Ed Baird – both of whom would have crossed us had we continued on port.

Fortunately, the breeze did go a bit more right. We crossed the red boat, whose stern we had ducked a moment ago, by about four lengths. Curtis came into the mark with a narrow lead over Coggan, who had reached down over us. We just made it up in front of Baird who had slightly overstood in the puff, and Allen slipped in on our lee-bow at the mark.

As we had practiced our spinnaker sets countless times, there was very little conversation at the windward mark. As Peter bore off, Tuck eased the jib, and Peter positioned the boat where he wanted it to be. In this case, with Allen just ahead and Baird right behind, we sailed a couple of boatlengths high before setting. "Okay," said Pete, "go for it!"

Once everything was set and flying, Tuck got into the chute trim, Pete worked on riding the waves and trimming the main, and I watched the boats around us and looked for the reach mark. "I can't find the mark yet," I said, "but Baird's going up, so work up about half a boatlength." A minute passed. "Okay, I've got the mark. We're a few degrees high, but we're okay right here." We were just to weather of Allen's wake and about two lengths behind him, and Baird had fallen in line behind us rather than forcing both us and Allen up to defend, which would let Curtis and Coggan extend their lead over all of us.

"Speed's good, Tuck," I said.

As the reach mark neared, "Let's get set up for the jibe," Pete said, then, "Okay, let's go."

After the jibe, I gave a reading on the situation. "The mark's off a bit, and

Baird's breaking low. Let's go down inside Allen." By staying to leeward and behind, Baird was signaling to us and Allen that he was not going to play games on this leg, and that all three of us wanted to work together to gain on the two leaders, and open the distance between us and the rest of the fleet. However, Baird worked extra low and with the help of a little lift and a lot of boatspeed, broke through to leeward of both Allen and us to move into third place at the leeward mark.

Up the next beat it was upwind business as usual, Pete and Tuck keeping our boatspeed up and I looking around at the other boats, the wind on the water, and the compass. "Okay, Pete, speed's good. Here comes a puff – it'll be a knock."

"Do you want me to tack just as it hits?" Pete asked.

"No, let's get into it a bit and see if it's holding," I replied.

As the puff hit, the proper adjustments were made, and I looked up ahead to see if the puff was lasting. It was. "Okay, Pete, pick your place and go." We ended up working the middle right side of the beat, while Baird and Allen slid off to the left. But I decided in this shifty breeze to sail our own beat rather than follow the other two. Fortunately, the last shift into the mark was a big right, and we had Baird by two lengths and Allen by ten.

On the run, Coggan and Curtis opened up a big lead, with Curtis ahead. Our strategy was to try to stay ahead of Baird and thus hold onto third place. Because the last shift into the mark was to the right, we did a jibe set, and for the rest of the run we tried to keep to Baird's left, which would leave us inside at the leeward mark. At one point Baird jibed to starboard. We went another four lengths or so before jibing in order to keep our air clear. When he jibed back onto port, we jibed inside, but due to his better downwind boatspeed, our lead at the mark was narrowed to one boatlength.

Once around the mark, Baird tacked immediately. At that moment we were on a port header, but starboard tack led right back into the bad air and wake of the rest of the fleet coming down the leeward leg with their spinnakers up. What to do? Because I've been burned too many times for not covering, we tacked, but then I made a fatal mistake – about a minute later, and still in the thick of the fleet's bad air and wake, we got a big header. Baird, to leeward, began to look better and better, but he didn't tack. In a header, the leeward boat doesn't cash in on its gain until it tacks, in which case, we would have tacked also to stay to leeward and ahead. But because Baird didn't tack, we should have kept going with him, waiting for the next lift. Oh well. We tacked right in the bad air and water, Baird went about 40 seconds farther tacked in clearer air, and pulled out to weather of us. From there on, he covered us up the beat. Every now and then we tacked off a lift, trying to get away from him a bit, hoping for a break. None for sale. Curtis and Coggan ended up one and two. Baird finished third, and we finished a close fourth just ahead of Allen.

CHAPTER 18

The Tactical Mind: Explored

WE WERE DRIVING to a major championship once where I was going to be the tactician, and the guy who was going to be steering asked, "Hey, what do you do in the situation where there's a boat about four boatlengths to windward of you and two back, and you want to tack; in other words, if you do tack they'd cross you by about two lengths and could easily tack on your wind? Do you tack and hope they don't tack on you, or do you just keep going, waiting for them to tack first?"

Though it may seem very simple on the surface, it's actually an intriguing and complex situation, and one that we run into all the time in the game of sailboat racing. For some situations, the answers are cookbook. For others, though, to get to the solution you have to go through an intricate maze of "do this if this happens, but do that if that happens." What I'd like to do is explore what goes on in the heads of tacticians when they're trying to solve these puzzles and illuminate the kind of thinking that should happen on board every boat playing the game.

THE FIRST STEP is to have a program that you put your information into. Before making your decision on what to do in a certain tactical situation, consider these four questions:

1. What are the *possible* next moves?
2. What are the *probable* next moves?
3. What would you *like* the next move to be, and can you affect it?
4. How will you *maximize your position* in each possible outcome?

Some situations come up over and over and, because you've been in them a lot, the answers to the questions, and therefore the right moves, come quickly. For instance you're on starboard, two boatlengths short of the starboard tack layline with about ten lengths to go to the windward mark. There's another starboard tacker up on your hip that you could tack and cross by two lengths. A port tacker comes across and tacks right on your wind. What's your immediate move? Obviously, to tack, go up in front of the other starboard tacker and tack back in clear air on the layline. You have this one down to a science because you used to try to hang on in bad air only to discover that as you went slower the starboard tacker to weather quickly moved up, suddenly closing the door and preventing you from tacking back without taking their stern.

Other situations, however, come up only now and then in a season, and as a result they take more time to figure out. The frustrating truth is that people who have raced more races against tougher competition will have encountered more situations and will be able to answer the questions and make the right moves faster.

But it doesn't have to be just that way. There are other things you can do to quicken your tactical reaction time. For those who are interested in improving their racing and like to play games, any situation that might come up on the course can be thought about on land. Just set up a situation and then take the place of each boat. What moves would one boat make, then what does the first do in response? Then go back and see if one or the other could have done something better or trickier to get the advantage. If you do this realistically, you'll already have figured out what to do and can act instantly. You'll also find that a lot of situations have no easy out, and you can keep an eye out not to get set up in them in the first place.

LET'S TAKE our first question as an example of the thought process going through a tactician's mind. "What do we do when we want to tack, but there's a boat to weather of us in a position to tack on our air when we tack?" (For the example both boats will be on starboard tack.)

1. When we tack, what can they *possibly* do?

    a. Cross and keep going.

    b. Cross and tack to weather, giving us clear air.

    c. Tack with us, finishing their tack to leeward and ahead.

    d. Cross and tack right on our air.

2. When we tack, what will they *probably* do? This is trickier to answer, but the best way is to put yourself in their position. Here are some considerations:

    a. What's the situation? Is it an obvious header you're tacking on, or is it a subtle strategy with a persistent shift, change of current, or something you've just noticed on the other side of the course?

    b. Are you getting near the layline?

    c. Who is in the other boat? Are they near you in the series, do they owe you any favors, will they camp on you just because you're one of the fast guys?

3. What would you *like* to have happen?

    Well, obviously you want to tack and go to the right in clear air, and depending on your strategy you may or may not want the other guy to come back across with you. Now, can you affect it? If you're getting near the layline, you can call to the other boat telling them that you're waiting for them to tack first. They'll then probably go near the layline and tack, leaving you slightly overstood but in clear air to weather when you tack. If you're in the middle but in a big header, you can call something to the effect of, "C'mon let's go, we're in a big knock!" However, this can easily backfire because some people get more of a kick watching you suffer than they do sailing a good race. Another move is to wait till they hit a big wave and then tack. Often by the time they're organized, you're already at their transom and in clear air when they tack.

4. After you tack, what will you do to *maximize your position* in each of the possible outcomes listed in (1)?

    a. If they cross and keep going, you're in fat city.

    b. If they cross and tack to weather, just keep a close read-out on their speed so they don't drive over you.

    c. If they finish their tack to leeward and ahead of you, sail fast and see if they're affecting your speed. If so, try to point higher (putting all your sail controls in their pointing gear), and if you're really slow, tack away, build speed, and tack back in clear air and water to weather.

d. If they land right on your air, you should already have decided if you want to bear off a few degrees into clean air or quickly tack, sail for a few lengths, then tack back in clear air to weather.

Of course, the question of whether to bear off or tack introduces a whole new situation, and before making your decision you'll want to put into the system all of the answers to the necessary questions, such as what will the wind do next, which side of the course is favored, how close to the mark? And so the game goes on.

HERE'S A SITUATION that comes up often: you're on port tack, about ten boatlengths downwind of the windward mark, and you're approaching the starboard tack layline with a boat to weather and behind. What's the best move?

Assuming that the boats are going to be close and that you want to try to beat them around the mark, going all the way to the layline is sealing your

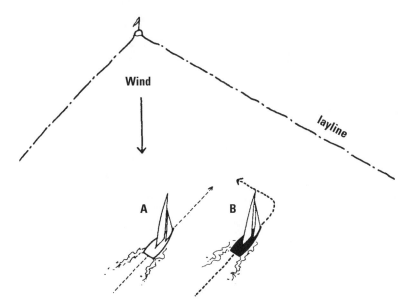

A and B are on port tack, about 10 boatlengths downwind of the windward mark. As they approach the starboard tack layline, B's best move is to tack three boatlengths short of the layline, and then to be prepared to deal with A's three possible responses.

The following are the three options:

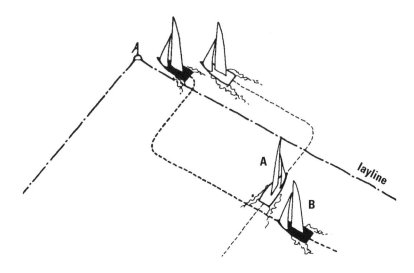

1. *If A crosses and continues, B should go all the way to the port layline and tack. If A overstands at all, B has a good shot at tacking inside. If not, B has lost nothing by trying.*

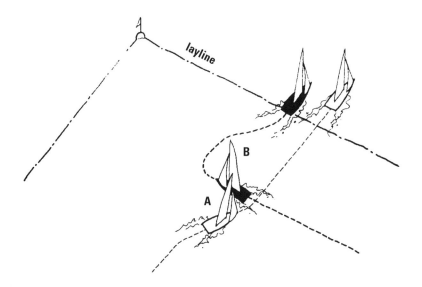

2. *If A ducks, B goes one length, tacks and reaches down to pin A to the right.*

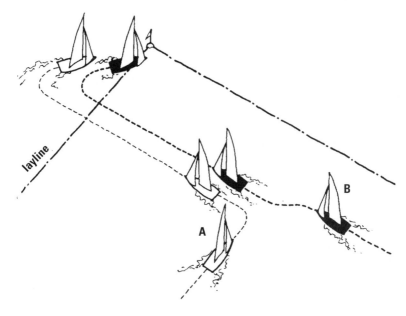

3. *If A can't cross, B should bear off slightly. If A lee-bows, B heads up and pins A past the port layline.*

fate. Any boat that's close can either tack in front of you or on your lee-bow and soon after pinch up between you and the mark. So try tacking three lengths short of the layline. If the port tacker just crosses you (they probably won't tack seeing you're not making it), you should go all the way and hit the port layline right on. Then assuming near equal speed and tacks, they have to hit their layline exactly to beat you. Because you have only a three boatlength layline to call, whereas they have much more, there's a good chance they'll overstand, in which case you probably will be able to tack inside them at the mark. If not, simply take their transom, tack, and you've lost nothing by trying.

If in the initial crossing the port tacker won't be able to cross you, crack off a few degrees as you approach (making sure not to break rule 16 by changing your course too close to them). If they decide to tack on your lee-bow, wait until they're head to wind and then trim back to close-hauled. Now pin them well past the port layline.

If they decide to duck, wait till their bow is at your transom, head up to close-hauled, sail for about one boatlength and tack (remember, you have a good head of steam on from being slightly cracked off). If they don't tack immediately quickly reach off and pin them to the right. If they do tack immediately, nestle a tight lee-bow under them while they're accelerating. Then by pinching and giving a series of sharp luffs, try to put them astern or force them to tack. If they tack and you're not definitely making the mark, tack back immediately to pin them to the right.

Now given all this, what would you do in this situation if you were the windward of the two port tackers coming toward the mark?

THE WHOLE RACE is a series of tactical episodes, a collage of situations and of situations within situations, each having its own circumstance and its own special way of being handled. Take, for example, the time we were racing Lasers at the Worlds in Australia. A friend was winning and I was about 20 lengths back in second, going up the last beat. Based on previous beats, the left was favored, and just about everyone was headed that way on starboard tack. I was well behind and out to weather (to the right) of my friend. Every time he tacked to port to try to cross me, I'd tack. Eventually, he'd go back to starboard to stay in touch with boats going left, and I'd tack back to weather. I was working left too, but I never let him cross my bow, thereby keeping the door open for Lady Luck to drop in. Sure enough, right at the finish he dropped into a hole and I got handed a big Puff Card from the right. Bullet.

Or how about the time Terry McLaughlin and I were racing for the win at the Snow and Satisfaction Regatta at Yale? It was whoever beat whom in the last race, and I led by three boatlengths off the weather end of the line. I expected Terry to flip to port as soon as he could clear the anchor line, but instead he hesitated for a second, then tacked. Just as I smugly tacked to cover, someone yelled and I looked back to see that we were tacking directly in front of a guy who had just borne off to duck our transom. In what was undoubtedly a spontaneous thought, Terry had lined us up beautifully and we had to tack back immediately – throwing us out of phase and into all kinds of bad wake and air. Terry went on to win the series.

Your tactical mind should be at work all the time, helping you pick the fastest lane at a toll booth, figuring out all the shortcuts around town and playing games like Parcheesi, Hearts, and my favorite, Stratego. Also, resail each race in your mind as soon as you can, searching for all the tactical situations that you encountered and figuring out how you got whaled on, how you handled someone else, and how you would have dealt with some situations differently. You'll find that your tactical bag of tricks will quickly grow and so will the fun you have playing the game.

CHAPTER 19

Understanding Windshifts

UNDERSTANDING AND PREDICTING windshifts is one of the most intellectual and important aspects of racing. Not even NASA scientists care whether the wind will shift five degrees in the next minute. But to sailors, this is a vital piece of information.

As a quick reminder, if a boat is sailing along and the wind shifts, forcing the boat to sail lower than it was previously, the boat has been headed. The opposite occurrence is called a lift. Given two boats, we all know that, in a header, the boat to leeward and ahead gains. (Just hold your hands straight out in front of you, and then cock your wrists to the left. Your hands are on starboard tack and your left hand has just pulled ahead.) But have you ever wondered how much the boat that was to leeward gains?

Unfortunately, one spring I did wonder, and my head is still tied up in knots. Nevertheless, thanks to the help of a good friend, Robert Hopkins, we succeeded in quantifying the exact gains and losses due to windshifts between any two boats anywhere on the race course, and the results are impressive. The method to my madness is to overemphasize the staggering importance of windshifts, in a day and age when more and more people are falling back on boatspeed and equipment excuses for poor finishes.

FIGURE 1 shows the geometric relationship of two boats sailing upwind. Notice that in a 10-degree header, Boat X gains 25 percent of the distance between her and Boat Y. If two boats go off the line even, on opposite tacks at the start of a mile-long beat, a quarter of the way up the leg they'll be one-half mile apart. One boat tacks so both boats are on the same tack. Going to Figure 3, at one-half mile apart (for boats that tack through 90 degrees), in a mere 10-degree shift one boat instantly gains 750 feet; for instance, in a head-

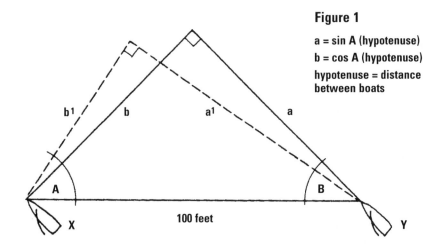

Figure 1

a = sin A (hypotenuse)
b = cos A (hypotenuse)
hypotenuse = distance
between boats

X and Y tack through 90 degrees. They are moving at identical speeds and are 100 feet apart (bow-to-bow). The solid-line triangle shows that if X were to tack (and lose no distance tacking), she would sail distance b; Y would sail distance a, and they would hit bow-to-bow. Because a equals b, they are even in the race.

In the dotted-line triangle, the wind has shifted 10 degrees to the left. Notice angle A has increased while angle B has decreased. However, the boats are still 100 feet apart. Also notice that the distance a^1 is now greater than distance b^1. By subtracting b^1 from a^1, we can determine exactly how much X gained.

er, if the boat to leeward and ahead tacks, she'll cross the other boat by one-eighth of a mile (which, in a 15-foot boat, is 50 boatlengths!).

If the breeze doesn't shift, it will take a boat going four knots twenty-one minutes to sail a one-mile beat. If one boat was going consistently one knot faster than another (which is highly unlikely in a small one-design dinghy), it would take seven and one-half minutes to gain 750 feet. If it was moving only half-a-knot faster, it would take over 15 minutes to gain 750 feet, or three-quarters of the leg.

Look at the figures for the five-degree shifts, which, if detected at all, are usually considered too trivial to tack on. At a mere half-mile separation, a 15-foot boat gains 24 boatlengths on an "inconsequential" five degree shift.

Figure 2 – Tacking through 80°

SHIFT	5°	10°	15°	20°	25°
ONE BOAT GAINS OR LOSES	11%	23%	34%	45%	55%

DISTANCE BETWEEN BOATS	DISTANCE GAINED OR LOST				
100'	10'	25'	35'	45'	55'
500'	55'	115'	170'	225'	275'
1200 ($^1/_5$ nautical mile)	130'	275'	410'	540'	660'
1500' ($^1/_4$ nautical mile)	165'	345'	510'	675'	825'
3000' ($^1/_2$ nautical mile)	330'	690'	1020'	1350'	1650'
Boatlengths gained or lost at $^1/_2$ mile separation (15' boat)	22	46	68	90	110

It's no wonder those corners look delicious; and it's even more amazing to consider the gain achieved from playing a shifty beat well.

Before getting to the meat of using windshifts tactically (see Chapter 20) it's imperative to understand why the wind shifts, and how to expect it to do what when. There are two kinds of windshifts that will alter the course of your boat: a geographic shift and a velocity shift, and it's critical to understand the difference. A geographical shift is when the wind blowing across the water actually changes direction. This is caused primarily by the weather system and local land masses. Dr. Stuart Walker's book *Wind and Strategy* and Allen Watt's books on weather forecasting are both excellent sources from which to learn why the wind shifts and how to predict it.

Geographic shifts fall into three patterns: persistent, oscillating, or random. In Newport, R.I., site of the 1980 U.S. Olympic Trials, the typical sea-breeze tends to shift steadily right as the afternoon goes on. This is an example of a persistent shift. In Newport, you can find also the classic Northwest-erlies. These cold-air systems move down across the continent and build up large, rhythmic oscillations. When they reach water, the winds will shift back and forth as much as 25 degrees every three minutes! Finally, if you've ever sailed on a small lake or enclosed harbor, you understand the random shifts. If not, come watch the Timme Angstens, the Rose Bowl of Intercollegiate Sail-

Figure 3 – Tacking through 90°

SHIFT	5°	10°	15°	20°	25°
ONE BOAT GAINS OR LOSES	12%	25%	37%	49%	60%

DISTANCE BETWEEN BOATS	DISTANCE GAINED OR LOST				
100'	10'	25'	35'	50'	60'
500'	60'	125'	185'	245'	300'
1200	145'	300'	445'	590'	720'
1500'	180'	375'	555'	735'	900'
3000'	360'	750'	1110'	1470'	1800'
Boatlengths gained or lost at $^1/_2$ mile separation (15' boat)	24	50	74	98	120

Figure 4 – Tacking through 100°

SHIFT	5°	10°	15°	20°	25°
ONE BOAT GAINS OR LOSES	14%	27%	40%	53%	66%

DISTANCE BETWEEN BOATS	DISTANCE GAINED OR LOST				
100'	15'	25'	40'	55'	65'
500'	70'	135'	200'	265'	330'
1200	170'	325'	480'	635'	790'
1500'	210'	405'	600'	795'	990'
3000'	420'	810'	1200'	1590'	1980'
Boatlengths gained or lost at $^1/_2$ mile separation (15' boat)	28	54	80	106	132

These figures are for boats tacking though 80°, 90° and 100°. They show the actual gains in feet (rounded to the nearest 5') that one boat makes over the other, both boats being even before the shift. For instance, in a 15-degree shift at a $^1/_4$ mile separation (for boats that tack through 90°), the boat that gains, gains 37% of their separation distance, or 555'! Notice that for closer-winded boats (Solings, Lasers, etc.) the gains and hence, losses, are less. Conversely, for more open-winded boats (420s in light air and chop), etc., the gains and losses are greater.

Example 1 – Starting from even: *(In each case the boats tack through 90°)*

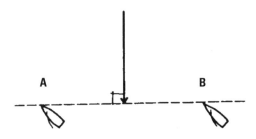

In the header, A gains the corresponding percent of the distance between the boats. B gains in the lift.

SHIFT	5°	10°	15°	20°	25°
LIFT (B GAINS)	12%	25%	37%	49%	60%
HEADER (A GAINS)	12%	25%	37%	49%	60%

Example 2 – Starting from when one boat is directly astern of the other:

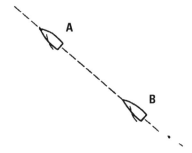

A gains in header. B gains in lift.

SHIFT	5°	10°	15°	20°	25°
LIFT (B GAINS)	9%	19%	29%	40%	51%
HEADER (A GAINS)	9%	16%	23%	28%	33%

ing, held each Thanksgiving in Belmont Harbor, just 100 yards east of Chicago's downtown skyline. Once, my crew and I literally sailed on a run up the middle of the beat, while boats on either side were still tacking upwind!

This, to me, is the most interesting diagram. It describes the percent of the distance between two boats gained or lost in any position on the course. Notice that the initial gains or losses are greatest when the boats are even

Example 3 – When one boat is directly downwind of another:

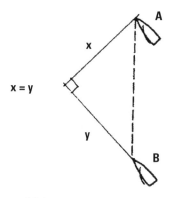

B gains in header and lift.

SHIFT	5°	10°	15°	20°	25°
LIFT (B GAINS)	*1%*	*3%*	*5%*	*9%*	*14%*
HEADER (B GAINS)	*1%*	*3%*	*5%*	*9%*	*14%*

Example 4 – When one boat is directly to leeward:

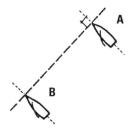

A gains in lift, B gains in header.

SHIFT	5°	10°	15°	20°	25°
LIFT (A GAINS)	*9%*	*16%*	*23%*	*28%*	*33%*
HEADER (B GAINS)	*9%*	*19%*	*29%*	*40%*	*51%*

(example 1) – for instance, right after the start and on the first beat. Also note that in example 2, a lift helps B more than the same degree header helps A. Also, in example 3, it's interesting that B, when directly downwind of A, gains in either shift.

The second type of shift that will alter the course of your boat is the velocity shift. For this you must understand apparent wind angles. Driving down the highway at 60 mph on a windless day, you stick your hand out of the window. Apparently, there is a 60 mph breeze blowing directly at the car. Your boat creates the same kind of headwind. To complicate matters though, your boat is also powered by wind blowing from another direction – the true wind direction. When sailing, the true wind and the headwind combine to form a third wind, somewhere in between the two in direction and slightly greater in force, called the apparent wind. This is the wind we set our sails to.

Picture this: anytime the boatspeed increases in relation to the true wind, or the true wind decreases in relation to the boatspeed, the apparent wind shifts forward, and the opposite is also true. Racing along, you sail into a hole or a lull in the breeze. Instantly the true wind decreases, whereas the boat's momentum keeps the boat speed up slightly longer. Thus the apparent wind shifts forward, forcing the skipper to bear off to keep the sails filled. But the actual wind has not shifted, and tacking on this header would lead to disaster!

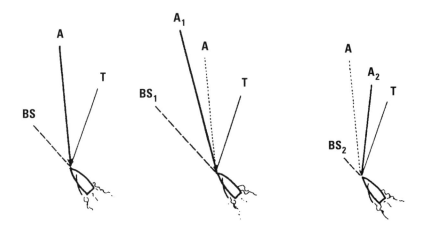

A = apparent wind, T = true (actual) wind, BS = the boat's speed

1) *The apparent wind (A) is a combination of the true wind (T) and the headwind caused by the boat's forward motion or boat speed (BS).*

2) *When the BS increases relative to the TW, or the TW decreases relative to the BS, the apparent wind (AW) shifts forward.*

3) *When the BS decreases relative to the TW, or the TW increases relative to the BS, the apparent wind (AW) shifts aft.*

THE KEY TO USING WINDSHIFTS tactically is being able to predict, with reasonable accuracy, what's going to happen to the wind at any point throughout the race. The better your information concerning the wind, the more accurate and precise your expectations become. Whenever I go to an unfamiliar place to race, I seek out the best local sailors (preferably, those who won't be in my race), and take them out for a couple of beers. Then, just mention a curiosity in the local conditions, and stand back! It's guaranteed that within the hour every napkin in the place will be filled with squiggly arrows and "do this if the wind does that" diagrams, turning you into a local practically overnight.

The next step is to get out on the water. Even if your boat and crew aren't ready, offer to go out with someone else or borrow a boat – even a motorboat. Take regular wind readings, time the shifts and watch the clouds to see how they affect the wind. Generally, a change in the sky indicates a forthcoming change in the wind. Look at the water, the waves, the direction of the ripples, the differing shades (sunglasses are excellent for this) and see if you can draw any conclusions. Then, try making predictions. As Lowell North says, "It's just a matter of practice. When you see a puff coming, guess how long it will take to reach you, and what the velocity and direction change will be. Then check yourself with what really happens. The guys who are good at this have just worked the process longer and harder."

Also, go near land masses, as they will always have an effect on the wind. Listen to the exciting VHF weatherband forecasters, particularly with regard to what clothes to have on board. Finally, as you get better, you'll want to call the local airport to find out what the wind is doing at different altitudes. Write all this information down, talk with others to get their impressions, and compare it to what the locals said. One fellow used to record what he learned on a cassette while driving home after regattas. Then the following year when getting ready to go sailing in the same place, he'd replay his last year's experiences.

On the day of the race, get out to the course about an hour before the race starts. Sail upwind on both tacks, writing down your compass headings and time of readings. This not only gives you an idea of the wind's pattern, but numbers to refer to on the first beat. Incidentally, be sure the size and quality of your compass does not increase solely with the size and cost of your boat, but rather with the seriousness of your racing. On my Laser, I used a large compass for its excellent dampening and readability.

Before the start, continually stand up in your boat to see what puffs are coming down the course. The higher off the water you get, the easier it is to see the breeze. During the race, get your head out of the boat. Continually look around and think all the time. Notice flags on stake boats at future marks, cruising boats in the distance (careful though, they fool you with their engines), the sky, the water, and other boats in your race. When I crewed for Bill Shore, we spent the entire two reaches analyzing the previous beat: who went where, what did and didn't pay, and why. Then we planned our strategy for the next beat based on our information, including the fresh experience of having just sailed it.

So it should be obvious by now that understanding wind shifts is critical, and the sailor who does his homework thoroughly will have the best feel of what to expect from the wind and, consequently, will have the most fun and success in using windshifts tactically.

CHAPTER 20

Tactics
in Windshifts

*"All my life, people tried to make tactics in
shifty breezes seem so complicated. Then I went
to Tufts University where coach Joe Duplin put
it like it is: 'Don't worry about all those fancy
shifts; just get your boat on the tack pointing
you closer to the mark and make that
scoundrel run for its life!'"*

– Jamie McCreary

TACTICS IN WINDSHIFTS is a subject nearly every author has taken
a shot at and, as a result, most sailors know what they should be doing on
the race course. However, having put in some serious corner time myself,
what interests me is the difficulty most of us have actually doing what we
know we should be doing.

It boils down to a simple mind game: you're racing upwind on port tack.
Suddenly, the four boats ahead of you tack, and almost simultaneously you
get headed. The unemotional and intellectual side of your mind says, "Tack
immediately! We'll be to leeward and ahead of the pack in clear air and going
fast toward the next header!" But the personality and ego side quickly coun-
ters with, "Hang on! We'll never pass those guys by following them. Keep
going, wait for a bigger knock and get'em all!" But by now it's too late to
tack without tacking right into a lot of bad air and wake, which even less inviting, so you keep on. Of course, the next thing to happen is a lift, putting
those four boats even farther ahead and leaving you waiting for an even big-

ger knock so that you can at least get back to where you started from. You keep on, and on, and on, until finally you pass a little sign in the water that says, "Welcome to Cornersville, Pop. 1."

It all boils down to several key barriers:

- Sailing is supposed to be fun, but most spell fun W-I-N. Our urgency and desire to win causes great pressure in and of itself, particularly when we've gone a while without winning. Our loss of confidence causes us to start taking more and more chances with boatspeed and tactics.

- Our ego and our need to be right controls many of us. It's very hard to fall in behind a pack, even if we know the pack is sailing in the correct direction. The tendency is to head off in the other direction, envisioning ourselves out in front and the heroes of the day.

- The frightening thing about the aforementioned scenario is the confident commitment that people make to it. This is due to the immense unpredictability of the weather, otherwise known as luck. It's often impossible to resist the temptation to wander off by ourselves with the hope that this is the day for the big break.

- Worrying about who the other competitors in the series are can be another serious barrier. Personally, I've always done my best when I've gone into a series not thinking I was going to win it. Overconfidence and lack of respect for my competition have always nailed me.

And, there are plenty of other factors that become barriers to clear, rational thinking:

- psych jobs in the parking lot, etc.
- rivalries and grudge matches from previous regattas
- bad vibes at a certain location where something went wrong before
- feeling that you'll make lots of mistakes, but that no one else will
- predetermining your finish in the regatta ("I'll probably finish in the mid-20s," etc.)
- psyched out by the weather – heavy air, chop, light air, etc.
- and the inevitable pressure in the last few races caused by a close series.

All of these and other factors mount up to prevent us from doing the one thing we want to do most – race sailboats as well as possible.

THERE IS A RATIONAL approach that will help overcome some of these barriers, particularly with regard to tactics in windshifts. A good gambler always seems to know when to shoot for it and, especially, when to fold. Undoubtedly, he knows the game well enough to assign odds and probabilities to each possible outcome. But most of all, he realizes the incredible importance of remaining conservative when the odds aren't good.

Back to the original example: you're sailing along on port; the four boats ahead tack, and almost simultaneously you get headed. If the breeze is oscillating, then the next shift will most likely be a port tack lift. Tacking immediately will put you in the safest position when the shift comes. You may gain slightly or just hold even, but you won't lose – high percentages move with good odds. However, the longer you hold on past the pack, the worse the odds in your favor get. Gamble as much as you dare, but as soon as you realize the gamble may not pay off, fold and tack back. Unfortunately, what usually happens is this rationalization: "Well, I'm behind already, and if I tack back now, I'll just be conceding my loss; so let's hang on a little longer and see if we get a big knock to go back on" – low percentages, bad odds.

So the rational approach to tactics in windshifts is to continually assign odds to certain possible outcomes throughout the race and execute where the odds are most in your favor. It might be that ten other boats are thinking the same as you, in which case you may follow a pack around the entire course. Or it may be that you decide to take a flyer, even though the odds of its working are extremely poor. The important thing is that you've thought about it, there's a reason behind each move you make, and you fully understand the odds of their success.

NOW, LET'S QUICKLY REVIEW some of the important tactical considerations when sailing upwind in an oscillating breeze.

Before the race, get a feel for the frequency and size of the oscillations and the strength and directions of the puffs and lulls (see Chapter 19). Force yourself to remember that the object of the first beat is not to be first at the mark. The object is to sail the shortest possible distance in the strongest wind and end up somewhere in the hunt. Unfortunately, you never know what that course is until after the beat's over. So, up the first beat, stick with the good odds, keep in touch with the bulk of the fleet and resist the temptation to go for it all.

Your primary race is against the wind. Don't let boats in front distract you. Use them to see what shifts are coming next. Start where you can get on the lifted tack immediately. Don't worry about sailing in bad air. The gains from hitting three consecutive ten-degree shifts are miles more than the four or five boatlengths lost in bad air. If you are in bad air and wake and going toward a header, drive off two or three lengths to clear your air. If going toward a lift, make two quick tacks.

The tactician's total energy must go toward positioning, and the key word is separation. The larger the separation between you and other boats, the larger the gains and losses will be. The closer you are, the less you'll lose and gain. Stay close to hang in there, get away to pass – simple! (see Chapter 19).

The more in the middle of the beat you are, the more open your options are: the closer to the layline, the fewer your options. Shifty breezes can be fickle, so continually drag yourself back to the middle. Don't necessarily wait for just five more degrees. Open your eyes, sail toward a puff and use the puff to take you back toward the middle. If you're right of middle on port, and getting headed, tack onto the starboard lift and get across to the middle as quickly as possible for the next header. Foot in the lifts, point in the headers

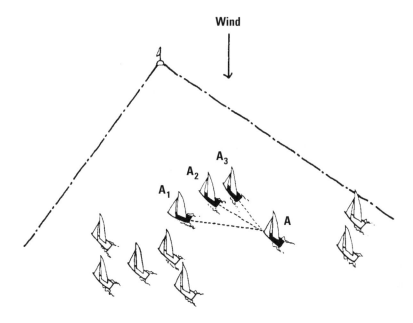

If you are A, sailing on a lift, do you:

A₁ – foot slightly, going faster through the water?

A₂ – sail a normal close-hauled course?

A₃ – or put the boat in point-mode, sailing higher but slower?

You should foot (A₁), putting yourself in the best position to use the next header.

(diagram). Tack back to leeward and ahead of boats coming in to the middle. This gives you more fighting room, more options, and you're less likely to be tacked on.

Watch the other boats to determine wind shifts (diagram). You don't actually gain on another boat until you're on converging tacks. As between two boats on port, the one to leeward and ahead gains in a header. But he doesn't actually realize the gain until he tacks over. If you can cross or get closer to a boat that was previously farther ahead, do it! Grind boats down little by little.

When the wind starts to shift, when should you tack? If the shifts are fast and frequent, tack immediately in a header. If the header is slow and gradual, tack halfway through it or at the mean (halfway between the most lifted and most headed course on that tack). Above all, be on the tack aiming you closer to the windward mark. If you're to leeward and ahead of some boats and

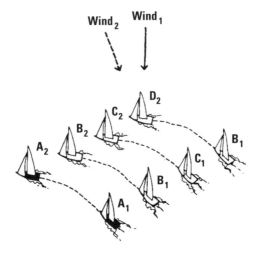

1) A is clearly behind B, C and D.

2) Now B, C and D appear to be slipping back. If boat speeds have remained constant, the wind is shifting to the left, heading the boats.

start to get lifted, decide what the odds are of the wind shifting back before you reach the layline. If good, hang on. If bad, tack back to windward (inside) of the boats.

Finally, here are some thoughts on boat-to-boat tactics in a shifty breeze. If you're on starboard going the way you want and a port tacker is approaching, wave him across your bow. That's much better than having him lee-bow you, forcing you to tack. If you're on port, ask starboard tackers if you should tack or cross. Chances are good they'll let you go. (Don't forget – rule 10 still requires you to keep clear). If you're on starboard or port and a boat is clearly going to cross you, pinch up to close the distance. This will delay or prevent them from tacking on you. And if they do tack on you, have it already figured whether you're going to drive off or tack to free your air, so you can react immediately. The elements that make the good tactical sailors great are:

    a. their ability to anticipate what's going to happen next

    b. their precision in assigning accurate odds to the various responses to what's going to happen next, and

    c. their reflex ability to react instantly and execute before the opportunity's gone. When sailing in shifty and puffy wind, you have to be thinking continually. Racing is a game of minimizing mistakes; good sailors don't make fewer mistakes than others, just smaller ones.

Probably the best way to improve your own consistency and finishes in shifty air is to watch a good series. When you can get out and look at the entire picture, even the smallest mistakes become obvious. You'll also get a good mental image of how the top guys attack the race. Most important, you'll get a much broader feel for the dynamics of the race course – the laylines, the effect of bad air, current effect, sail shapes, etc. – much more than you could ever get inside your boat.

Tactics in windshifts are frustratingly fundamental on paper, yet deceptively difficult to apply consistently. Just for fun, pick a series and plan to sail it the way you know you should be sailing it. Who knows – it might be the best chance you ever took.

CHAPTER 21

The Tactical Mind: Strategy

ONE OF THE REASONS why sailing is such a complex and fun game is that you're not just racing against the other boats, you're also testing your ability to sail the fastest path around the course. Go out and watch any race and you'll be surprised to see how often people give up inches and feet in their travels around the buoys. Some are lost through carelessness in obvious situations like mark roundings, tacks, etc. Others slip away more subtly. So for the moment let's forget about all those other boats and look at some strategies for simply trimming excess fat off our own trip around the course.

Choosing the Right Tack Shortly After the Start

Before the start, you'll obviously want to have a reasonable idea of what you expect the wind to do based on your own knowledge or by talking to the best locals. It really helps to take repeated wind checks to see what sort of oscillations you have to play with. Also notice if one tack will take you closer to a shore. More times than not, that tack will be favored.

Also look to see where the committee sets the windward mark and figure out if you'll be spending more time on one tack than the other on your way to the mark. One common misconception is that if the windward mark is not set directly upwind from the starting line, it affects which end of the line is favored. For instance, if the line is set square to the wind, but the windward mark is 100 yards to the left of being directly upwind of the line, then boats starting at the left end of the line will sail a shorter distance to get to the mark. This is absolutely wrong.

If the line is set perpendicular to the wind direction, then all the boats starting anywhere on the line will be mathematically even at that point; and if the

Wind

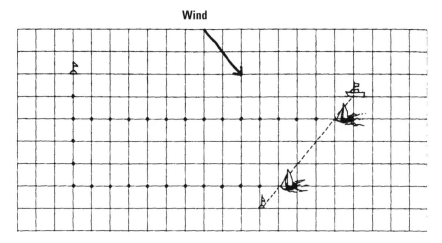

One common misconception is that if the windward mark isn't perfectly upwind of the line, then the end of the line closest to the mark is favored. However, as long as the line is set perpendicular to the wind, boats starting at either end will be geometrically even in the race and will sail the same distances to get to the first mark. The difference is that one boat will sail more distance on one tack versus the other.

wind doesn't shift they will all sail the same distance to get to the mark (see diagram). The only difference is that boats starting at the left end of the line will sail less time on starboard tack than the boats starting at the right end. As a good general rule, it pays to sail the longer tack first after the start, at least until you're directly downwind of the mark. From then on you'll have equal sailing time on both tacks.

Getting Lifted on the Layline – Should You Take the Lift or Foot off for the Mark?

For some reason this has happened to me a lot recently, and it's a tricky situation. You're on the layline with a few minutes sailing to do to get to the mark, and you start getting lifted. If you follow the lift, you'll be overstanding and sailing away from the straight line to the mark. If you ease your sheets and head straight at the mark, you'll be sailing the shortest possible course at the moment. But if you crack off and the wind heads you 15 degrees, you won't make the mark, costing you a minimum of two more tacks and a longer sailing distance to get there.

One thing to remember is that all boats react differently when you crack them off ten or so degrees, especially in strong winds. Crack a 470 off ten degrees in 20 knots, and it will start planing wildly. Crack a Soling off the same ten degrees in the same 20 knots, and it will just heel over and stop.

So when lifted on the layline, my strategy is now based on the kind of boat I'm in. If the boat will go the same speed or faster cracked off for the mark than it would sailing close-hauled, then I'll head down to just slightly above the mark and trim the boat for that course. The advantages are:

- You're sailing a shorter distance than the boat taking the lift.

- If the wind heads you, so that you're closehauled again on the layline, you're right back where you started, and the boat to weather of you has overstood.

- If you get headed below the layline, you'll gain on the boats to weather and behind.

- If the wind does head you, reaching through the lift will close the distance between you and the boats to leeward, thereby reducing your loss in the header.

On the other hand, if I think my boat will go slower cracked off than close-hauled, I'll take some of the lift until it becomes obvious that the breeze won't shift back before I round the mark. Then, of course, you have to head for it. I'll also take the lift if I notice the lifts are puffs and that the farther to weather I get, the sooner I'll get the breeze.

Being Headed on a Tight Reach under Spinnaker –
Should You Drop or Carry the Chute?

This situation also comes up frequently and is especially a problem in heavier winds. You're planing down the first reach with the chute up and you notice that you aren't holding high enough for the jibe mark. Your options are to trim everything hard and try to head higher; bear off, ignore the mark and sail fast; or drop the chute and sail under main and jib.

Based on experience, my first strategy would be to sail as high as possible under the chute, keep the pole forward and up, and trim hard on the sheet, but still keep the leading edge curling religiously every two or three seconds. If the jib is also up, you should keep it well eased and be sure the clew is as far outboard as physically possible so it doesn't interfere with the chute trim. Unless it's windy, keep the main powered up, i.e. traveler up, outhaul eased, backstay eased, etc. If it's windy, depower the main so the boat doesn't heel or broach, i.e. backstay on, vang completely off, cunningham on as hard as possible, outhaul tight, etc. In this case you may choose to keep the traveler up and play the sheet out for maximum twist up top.

If you still can't make it, the general rule is to bear off and sail the boat with the chute as fast as possible until you reach the point where you'll go the fastest on a jib reach. Then drop the chute and reach up to the mark. If there's a chance the wind will lighten or shift aft, drop the chute to leeward and leave your pole on so you can reset quickly. If you're certain you won't be resetting on that leg, drop it to weather so you can set it from the leeward side after the jibe for the second reach.

Current

Racing in current is always tricky business, especially for those of us who don't get the pleasure very often. One misconception about current, which took a friend of mine, Peter Isler, about a year of patient hammering to point out to me, is that there is no lee-bow effect. I was brought up believing that if you were heading right into the current, your boat would be slowed, but that if you angled your boat so that the current was on your lee-bow it would push you nicely to weather. Peter finally parted my clouds so that now I see that current can't push the boat through the water. Current is the movement of the water itself, and because our boats are simply floating on the water, the current will always try to move us in the direction it's going, regardless of which way we're heading. Just picture a stick floating down a river. It will float just as fast and in the same direction whether it's lined up with the flow of the river or turned sideways to it.

The bottom line to all this is: in current don't alter the way you sail your boat. Of course the current is moving your boat through the air and will cause its own wind, but this wind effect is automatically built into your apparent wind. The only time you might alter your angle of sail in current is when you feel you're in favorable current but are slowly sailing out of it. Then you may choose to pinch slightly or tack to stay in the current; or if you're in strong adverse current with weaker current ahead, you may choose to foot to get out of the stronger current sooner.

The current will also affect your strategy when it comes time to round the marks. If the current is flowing from left to right, and you're on starboard tack and not quite making the windward mark to be left to port, pinch your boat so you go slower straight ahead through the water. If you plan it well, the current will carry you to the right of the mark, before you get to it. This eliminates the need for making two tacks to round the mark, which in many boats is slower than pinching for twenty seconds. You have to know your boat.

Also, current will change your laylines. If the current is flowing directly downwind, you will have to go farther on port before tacking to starboard to make the weather mark. The best strategy here, assuming the current strength is even over the area, is to go all the way to the port layline, tack, and come by the mark as close as possible. This gives you the shortest possible amount of starboard tack sailing time and therefore the easiest call as to when to tack.

The Corners and the Rhumb

One of the easiest places to trim off excess inches is at the turning marks and on the reaches. The straight line between any two marks is called the rhumb line, which is, of course, the shortest geometric distance between two points. But even in the absence of current and puffs, people carelessly wander away from the rhumb on reaches. Before rounding any mark, you should find the next mark. To help you find the next mark, take time out before the start to notice any distinguishing reference points on land behind the area of the mark – the condominiums on shore will always be easier to find than the light blue hippity-hop anchored half a mile away.

Also, when sailing down the reaches, be very sensitive to your position relative to the rhumb line. Don't ride waves high of the rhumb unless you're sure

Wind

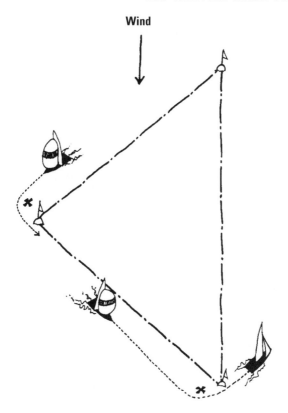

When rounding the jibe and leeward marks, turn around imaginary marks so that you will finish your turn as you pass the real mark. When practicing, try to touch the mark with your hand after you have jibed or headed up to close-hauled.

you can catch some to bring you back down. When a puff hits, don't go blindly zooming off on a screaming plane ten degrees high of the rhumb, because you'll find that when the hose is finally turned off and you can see again, you may have to sail an embarrassingly slow broad reach to get back down to the mark. Any waves or puffs that will carry you below the rhumb are gravy because you will only go faster when you reach up to the mark. So on the reaches, dig in and don't stray half a boatlength above the rhumb line unless you have to.

To ensure you're sailing the straightest possible course to the mark, especially in current or strong wind where boats make considerable leeway, watch the land behind the mark. If the mark appears to be drifting to the right against the land, then you are slipping to the left, and you have to head more to the right. If the mark is not moving against the land, you are right on track. So don't simply aim at the mark; watch the land behind it to be sure it's holding the same.

When it comes time to turn the marks, remember that most boats lose speed in sharp turns. If you're coming into a jibe mark to be left to port, and you're on the starboard tack, don't sail directly to the buoy. The goal is to be able to jibe the main, then be able to reach out and touch the buoy with your hand. This means jibing around an imaginary mark about half a boatlength to weather of the real mark (diagram previous page). The same applies at the leeward mark. Plan to round an imaginary mark half a boatlength to the right and slightly below the real mark. Here the goal is to be able to touch the mark after your sails and boat are trimmed for your closehauled course. In both cases, if you can't touch the mark, you've given up some critical feet on your turn.

Armed with some of these strategic suggestions, go out and watch a race. Note all the places people give up distance around the course, mentally add up how many boatlengths they've lost, and then watch how close most of the boats are at the finish. In most fleets saving ten boatlengths around the course can mean the difference between finishing fifth and 15th in the race – not bad for being just a bit more sensitive and careful.

CHAPTER 22

The Tactical Mind: Tricky Stuff

*We had just come off the line in the second race of the
1979 Soling Olympic Pre-Trials and were in pretty good shape,
headed right on port tack. The breeze was around eight knots.
All of a sudden there was a loud noise, and the main began
luffing. I whipped around from my middle crew position to
see the mainsheet ratchet dangling on the sheet. The clevis pin
holding it on had come loose, and as it slipped out, the shackle
holding the ratchet had bent open. My first idea was to trim in
and hold the main while Tucker, our forward crew, fixed the
ratchet. But Peter, who was skippering, was way ahead of me.
He had already grabbed a pair of vise-grip pliers from the
tool bag, and as I trimmed in the main, he tightly clamped
the vise-grips onto the sheet just as it exited the block on
the boom. It held beautifully, leaving Tucker free to trim
the jib, balance the boat, and look around, while I
fixed the unit.*

SAILING BY THE BOOK, avoiding the big bummers, and mastering the little things will zoom you to the top in short order, but once there, you begin to notice that the champs have yet another chapter in their repertoire of ways to beat you – a whole collection of tricky stuff. They may have used some of these tricks only once or twice in their career. Other moves and their variations, though, are subtly applied very frequently and are more noticeable once you know what to look for. Here's some of the trickier stuff I've run into over the years.

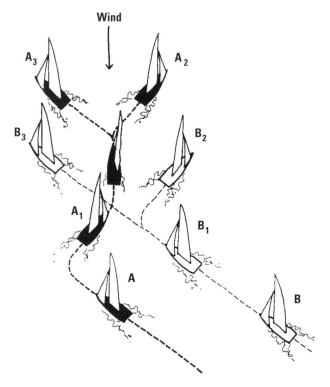

A wants to go right and wants B to go right as well. So, A tacks, crosses B by about three boatlengths, and then begins a slow tack back in front of B. If B tacks while A is tacking, A can fall back onto port. If B holds on, A completes her tack and tightly blankets B until B is forced to tack.

Around the Start

- If there's no land or any anchored boats to get a good line site on, sail outside of the right hand end of the line and come in on starboard so the two ends are in line with each other; then read your compass heading. Suppose it reads 090 degrees. Then, when you're in the middle of the line with one minute to start, and you're aiming at the pin on starboard, and your compass reads 110 degrees, you know you're well below the line. Or, let's say you're in the middle and want a quick reference to see how close to the line you are. Quickly bear off to 090 degrees. If you are right on the line, your bow will be aiming at the pin. If you're aiming to the left of the pin, you're obviously below the line.

- When you're starting near the left end, and that end of the line has a boat anchored with people sighting the line, it's helpful to figure out which person is calling the line and then watch their line of sight to get an idea of where the line is. You can figure they're looking directly toward the right end, so if they're not looking at you, you're probably still behind the line.

- If you had a nice hole to leeward of you, but are too close to the line, or if you want to kill time without getting any closer to the boats to leeward, an effective move is to luff your jib, keep your main trimmed tight, and then radically bear off and head up again. If you practice this a few times, you'll see that the boat can turn quite sharply in a small place, and by reducing your speed you won't travel too far leeward. To turn this into a killer move, you also have to know exactly how long it takes, how much room you need, and what is the fastest way to accelerate again when you have come to a near standstill.

Up the Windward Legs

- If you are to leeward and slightly ahead of another boat, and you want to tack, put all your controls in their pinching mode, i.e. travelers up, downhauls off, slightly more heel, etc. Then scallop your way up under the other boat until you've got them in your dirt. If they still won't tack, heel your boat slightly to weather, or pull down hard on your main leech and, either way, you will almost completely shut off their clean air supply.

- If you are slightly to windward and abeam of another boat, and you want to tack, but you want the other guy to come too, ease your sheets, bear off slightly until you are out in front of him, then trim in sharply. When he tacks, go another two lengths so he has plenty of clear air and then tack.

Near the Windward Mark

- If you're focusing on beating one boat near the end of a windward leg, decide which layline is closer. Then cover that boat toward it and camp

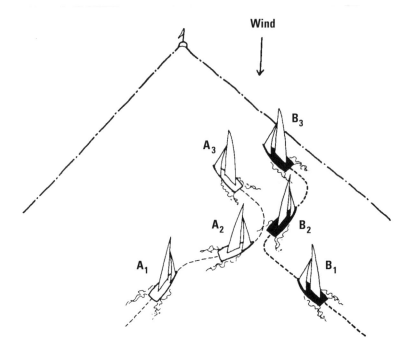

This situation between two boats near the windward mark comes up all the time. If A ducks B, A will have the starboard advantage coming back. B, though, is in the best tactical position to beat A around the mark. If the two boats are close to the starboard layline, then B should let A dip her stern and then tack immediately after A's bow has crossed her transom, pinning A out past the starboard layline. If over a minute of sailing is left on port tack, B should wait until A begins to bear off and then try to tack directly in front of, or slightly to leeward of A. B is not obligated to hold her course simply because A has borne off in anticipation of ducking her stern. However, if B's change of course forces A to immediately change her course to avoid B, then B has broken rule 16.2. But the moment B is on her new closehauled course and she is clear ahead or to leeward, A must keep clear. Once B is in there to leeward of A, B can pinch or luff, forcing A into her bad air or into a tack. If A tacks, B tacks immediately and pins A out past the port layline.

right on their wind when they try to tack away. Once they're at the layline the game's pretty much up, and you can sit on their air all the way to the mark. Of course if you ever find yourself at the layline with a boat to weather, ready to pounce on you when you tack, simply wait until they tack first. If there are other boats in the race, your predator will probably tack soon enough, and though you won't pass them, you'll sail to the mark in clear air and will have given up the least amount of distance possible.

- If you're heading for the mark on starboard, short of the layline and several boats are going to cross in front of you, it's often better to let them tack first and commit to their positioning before you tack out again. This way you'll know precisely where to tack relative to the layline to have the most clear air as you approach the mark.

- On the other hand, if you're approaching the windward mark on starboard, slightly below the layline, and there are boats on port passing behind you, or starboard tack boats nearby up to weather who are tacking back out to the layline, tack out immediately yourself. By staying close and to windward, you can safely tack in front of them or on their leebows and thus be assured of beating them to the mark. If you hold on and wait to come in on port, you're likely to get burned (as I have too many times), because they've gotten a slight lift or moved up while sailing in clearer air.

At Leeward Marks

- If you're the outside of two overlapped boats coming into a leeward mark to be left to port at the end of a run, there are a couple of moves you can pull to beat the other guy around. If you're both on starboard, try to crowd the inside guy as close as he'll slide toward the mark. Then, at the last moment, swing wide and execute a perfect jibe and roundup. If your friend inside blows his, cruise by on the inside. If both boats are coming in on port, you can try the same. Be sure to begin quietly slipping back so that only your bow is overlapped with his stern at the mark. Then swing out and wait to see if he blows his rounding.

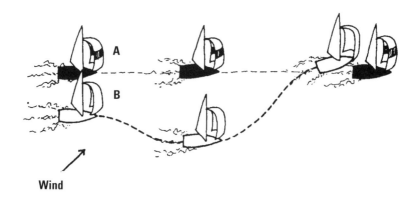

Wind

To pass A, B swings wide or slows down, then lets her main out and sails by the lee down A's transom wake to A's inside. To defend, A either heads up when B swings wide to keep B securely overlapped, or bears off sharply before B does, to widen the gap between them.

A's defense options:

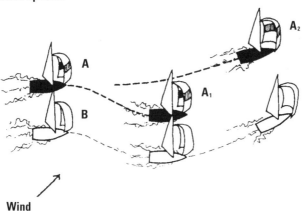

Wind

- Also keep your eyes out for any starboard tackers which have tacked right around the mark (see diagram 3). As the leeward boat you have the right to sail your proper course, and if you so choose, you can go astern of the starboard tacker. By doing so, you can often get your bow farther ahead coming into the mark; then, with a smooth turn, you can keep your bow out front once you're closehauled, putting you in the lee-bow position to gas your friend immediately.

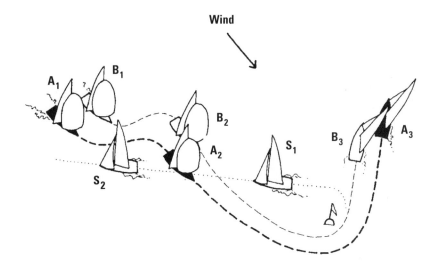

- If you're rounding close behind someone, it's often better to plan to round three-quarters to a full boatlength behind rather than right on their stern. Usually tacking immediately is slow due to all the congestion at the mark. The means you must hang on for at least half a minute or so. I've found it's tougher to pinch and hold high when you're directly astern of someone than when you have a bit of space between you. Also, by planning to leave the space, you'll never get caught overlapping them to leeward if they hit a wave or try some tricky stuff on you.

- Often you'll be rounding the leeward mark with a guy right on your tail. You can buy yourself a couple of bonus boatlengths with this move: come into the mark at full speed so the guy behind you is flying also. Then right before the mark, put your board down, radically overtrim your main, move aft, etc., so the boat quickly slows down. The idea is to force them to solidly overlap you to leeward as you round. Then they'll either be trapped there by boats rounding behind them or they'll have to tack immediately, sailing slowly in the bad air of the boats still coming downwind behind you. You can also achieve this effect by coming around the mark normally with them hot on your tail and then luffing sharply as soon as you clear the mark. They'll be forced to overlap to leeward, at which point you can bear off and gas them.

Other Tricky Stuff

Tucker Edmundson taught me a good one for when you need to lead a spinnaker sheet around your bow. Rather than clomping up on the foredeck to bring it back by hand, simply coil all the line up and toss it around the forestay from the windward side. As the line hits the water, the boat has already moved up to it, and you merely have to go to leeward to pick the sheet out of the water.

Building your own repertoire of tricky stuff comes from racing against the best competition as much as possible, always keeping a close eye on what the other top people are doing on the water and off, and whenever possible, sailing for at least one series (usually as a crew) with the people you respect the most in your area.

KEY YOUR EYES AND EARS OPEN, and stay in an aggressive, playful mood, always looking for the opening to pull a fast one as in the third race of the 1981 IYRU World Youth Sailing Championships when U.S. representatives John Shadden and Ron Rosenberg were involved in a very close race with an excellent team from Spain. The two were one-two in the race, well out in front of the rest of the fleet, with John and Ron trailing coming into the jibe mark. By continually working high, John had forced the Spanish team high to defend, and both teams had already jibed to port as they came into the reach mark about one boatlength apart. At the last second, Fernando, the Spanish skipper, looked back to make sure John didn't try to sneak inside. John immediately noticed that Fernando was aiming very close to the mark, so he headed up suddenly as if he were going for the pass. Instinctively, Fernando headed up also, but unfortunately for him, he ran straight into the buoy! Ahh, that tricky stuff. Well, at least there's one sailor out there who won't fall for that one again. And so the game goes on.

CHAPTER 23

Going for It Downwind: The First Reach

THIS IS THE FIRST of three chapters on racing downwind. In this chapter I will cover the tactics and strategy on the first reach of a triangular course, Chapter 24 will cover the second reach, and Chapter 25, the run. For many sailors, the fastest thing out of the bilge around the weather mark is still an ice-cold brew. But these chapters will, I hope, illuminate many of the tactical advantages that can be had downwind, so people can have more fun, and keep the pedal to the medal all the way around the race course.

Racing downwind is an entirely different game from the "let's all split in every direction conceivable" game we play on the beats. Because of this we must learn to use a whole new repertoire of tactics and strategy. The downhill game is much more straightforward, like football's offensive/defensive setup, with its "if they do this, we'll do that" type of strategy. In football, among good teams, both sides usually know what type of play to expect next. So the bottom line becomes not which team can be fancier, but which team can execute their plays better; and the real gains and losses, and often the most exciting moments, come from the errors.

Racing downwind fits this setup exactly. Only a certain number of different situations can arise, and each one has only a couple of moves to consider. The key is to be able to anticipate which situation will arise next, and position yourself ahead of time to take full advantage of it as it develops. In order to do this you must know all the situations that might arise, and why, and know all the offensive and defensive moves available to you. If you don't, you will undoubtedly be the one making the errors that will cost you distance and boats downwind.

Let's start by looking at the dynamics of the first reach. One thing about reaching is that everybody has to go more or less in the same direction and get to the next mark. This keeps the boats on the same tack and in a relatively straight line, making the tactics much simpler. What makes the dynamics of the first reach different from those on the second, is that on the first reach, a boat's "inside" side is opposite from the windward side.

Let's say the marks are to port. On the first reach the boats will be on starboard tack. Now you're zipping along, riding the waves nicely, and you start catching up with the guy in front of you. You have four options, one of which is to crash right into him, which won't really help the program any. The second is to slow down and fall in behind him. The third is to overlap him to windward, and the fourth is to overlap to leeward. The nice thing about overlapping him to windward is that you may be able to take his wind and pass him. But he has an easy defense if he chooses to use it – a good sharp luff (as long as he gives you room to keep clear under rule 16.1, Changing Course) – with which most sailors can keep another from going by to windward.

However, if you take the fourth option and overlap him to leeward, you'll probably be able to establish and maintain an inside overlap, and be entitled to room at the jibe mark. This is a great way to pass a boat, as there is very little they can do to defend against your attack. (On the second reach, however, the inside and windward side become the same, making the inside much easier to defend. This fundamental difference between the two reaches sets up a series of different tactical situations.)

TO EXPLORE THE TACTICS and strategy of the first reach, let's break it up into three sections: 1) the opening setup (first 200 feet or so); 2) the long midsection; and 3) the close (last 200 feet before the jibe mark). A lot of errors are made in the opening setup of the first reach. The two most important ingredients are speed and position. As you round the mark, it's imperative to keep the boat going at full speed. The classic mistake is that people round the mark, and instantly their heads are in the bilge doing the 101 things that must happen then. A way to increase concentration on speed after the mark, is to do as much as possible before you get there – i.e., ease the cunningham, outhaul, and vang; have the chute all hooked up; have the pole on; open the bailers; be sure there are no knots in your main and jib sheets (funny how those slip in there); ease the backstay, etc. The minimal loss in speed over the last 15 lengths into the mark as you make each of these preparations smoothly and efficiently will be far outweighed by the gains you make as you round the mark with the jib eased and the boat flat, catch that first wave, and take off.

In addition, you'll be able to concentrate much more on your critical positioning to start the reach. If you find yourself rounding the mark with no one within five boat-lengths of you ahead or behind, then it's safe to bear right off to the rhumb line (which is the straight line to the next mark). But if you find yourself rounding in a crowd, you have to decide immediately whether to head high or low initially. The only time I consider going low initially is when there is a pack in front of me, and a large space behind me. Then I can anticipate that people in the pack will luff each other higher and higher in an effort to break free, and that by sailing the rhumb line or lower I can sail a shorter, faster course and gain on the group.

But the risks from diving low initially are very high. If you round with a boat right on your tail and bear off sharply, you make it very easy for them to hold a tad higher and with their extra speed, roll you. Once they roll you, it could be a nonstop roll job for as long as there are boats in the neighborhood. So, in general, in crowds it pays to head high initially, and then play the reach from there. This is especially true when you have to set a spinnaker. The game is to use your speed to roll out to weather of the boats ahead whose spinnakers are halfway up and luffing. Then when you're well to weather and ready, calmly set your chute. Very often you can take their air and roll right over them.

Once free of the congestion near the mark, here's a guide for your overall tactics and strategy on the leg. The key consideration on the reaches, which are essentially follow-the-leader legs, is the physical distance between you and the leaders of the race, not how many boats happen to occupy that distance. Your whole strategy should be to reduce that distance as much as possible by the end of the two reaches, so that it's easier to go to work to pass them on the beat. If you happen to pass a few boats on the reaches, that's great, but that should not be your main strategy.

Now, to start reducing that distance you can't be passive. You have to get aggressive and be a little playful right from the start. Here are some ideas. If

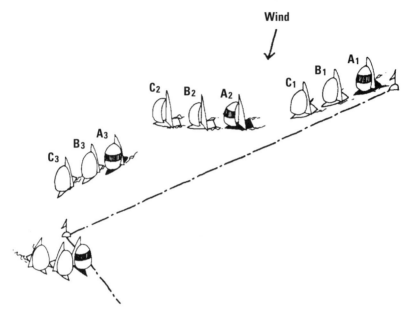

A₁ – *Boat A heads up slightly and boats B and C head up to defend.*

A₂ – *Boat A holds above rhumb line, working B and C higher.*

A₃ – *All three boats head for the mark. A captures the overlap on B, who has the inside overlap on C. A rounds ahead.*

you're a boat-length or so directly behind someone, and start to head higher, the response of that boat will generally be to head up also to defend against your passing to windward. But because they are sensitive to getting too high and allowing you to overlap them to leeward and inside, they will be cautious about how high they go. So start a little trouble when you're five lengths back. Head up a bit as if you're going high and watch for the boat ahead to defend. Then as they go up you find a nice little wave and ride it down. Their response will immediately be to work down again, at which time you go back up. This works, because all the time you are looking forward, riding the waves and puffs up and down, your friend ahead is frantically looking back and forward, trying to defend both his windward and inside side at the same time. If he doesn't go berserk first, it's almost guaranteed that the fellow ahead will overreact each time, especially if he turns the lookout duty over to a slightly hyperactive crew: "He's going up... he's going up! No wait, he's down... he's down!" This exact situation led the great Finn sailor, Henry Sprague, to glue a rear-view mirror to his boom.

By carefully working the wind and water you can easily gain big distance on the guy ahead. Besides, if you are behind a string of boats, the effects of your steering will cause a chain reaction as far ahead as the boats are in line, and each fellow ahead will overreact a bit more than the guy behind. A great way to scoop a handful of boats at once is to work the whole gang high, then as the group turns down for the mark, you grab the inside overlap (see diagram previous page).

Another great feeling on a reach is to have about a six-length jump on the next guy, and then watch as he has to head up to defend against boats behind him. Who can resist the urge to bear away a bit as your lead gets bigger and bigger? The truth is, good sailors work together to minimize the distance they lose on the leaders and to pull away from the boats behind; just as in professional stock car racing, it's not uncommon to see two guys, one slipstreaming the other, locked together and pulling away from the rest.

For example, you're in third, one length behind the guy in second. The leader is eight lengths ahead. You decide you'd like to move into second, so you head up a bit. Instantly, you are forcing the second place boat to head up and defend. Now assuming the guy's not a total space case, he'll be able quite easily to keep you from passing him to weather. But the longer and sharper you go up, the more he has to also. Finally, if you overlap him to weather, he has no choice but to luff you good and hard until you break it off. So often I've heard the guy behind in this situation telling the leeward guy he's an S.O.B. for luffing him to the moon. Wrong. It's the guy behind who controls the action. Meanwhile, in our example, you're still in third, the leader has opened to an insurmountable 16-length lead, and three more boats, previously way back, have moved up to within striking range on the next beat.

Now, if you see that you are closing fast on someone and want to pass him to weather, there's only one sure way to do it. You have to get up in the passing lane, which is two to three boat-lengths to windward of the boat to be passed, and you have to get there at least six lengths ahead of time. The closer astern you get to a boat, the easier and more enticing it will be for them to defend. Make your move early, get up in the lane, and when you do get clos-

Wind

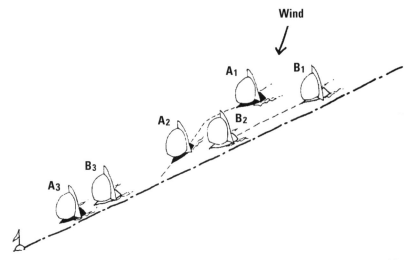

From A₁ to A₂, A sailed below her proper course. Since B was a leeward boat within two boatlengths of A, A fouled B under rule 17.2.

er, your victim will probably consider you too far to weather to bother with.

Likewise, if you are getting rolled, there are only two moves to make. If you can luff, then do it hard being sure they have room to respond (rule 16). One sharp luff is worth a thousand little ones, and usually disposes of the matter immediately. If a boat is going to pass that close to you they deserve to get luffed hard; and the last thing you want to engage yourself in is a one-on-one battle that takes you right off the race course. But if they do get your wind, come off and let them go quickly. At the same time, try to hop onto their leeward wake and slipstream along for a while. If they're going that fast, you might as well join 'em. Also notice anything they're doing differently that might help your speed – i.e., sail trim, boat trim, weight placement, board placement, steering, etc.

The key then to this midsection of the first reach is to minimize the distance you lose on the leader and open up on the guys behind. If a boat behind you starts to go up, you have to decide if it's an offensive or a defensive maneuver. If it's offensive, then decide whether you think they have a realistic chance to pass you. If so, head up a bit to defend and let them know either verbally, or with a sharp luff, that you understand what's going on. If they have boats going up behind them, then perhaps they're simply defending, in which case you can squeeze even closer to the rhumb line and extend your lead. As for trying to pass on the reach, be patient, use the passing lane, and try it only when you're sure it will work.

Now for the close. There's no advantage, and in fact a huge disadvantage, in being caught on the outside (windward side) of a group of boats near the jibe mark. The best strategy is to try to work down across the transoms to the inside of the boats around you and to break all overlaps of boats inside of you.

You'll want to begin working down well before the mark, and as you enter the last 200 feet or so, you can more often afford to let a boat move out to weather on you without wasting the distance to defend, as they'll have to climb up, pass over you, and come back down having broken the overlap – something which takes a while to do.

CHAPTER 24

Going for It Downwind: The Second Reach

THE DYNAMICS on the second reach of a triangle are different from those on the first, mainly because on the second reach a boat's windward side is also its "inside" side. Thus we have only one side to defend, and most of us do it with passion. The typical scene on second reaches all over the world is for the fleet to climb way out to weather of the rhumb line, only touching down again at the leeward mark. Armed with this vital tidbit of knowledge, let's explore the different tactics and strategies we can apply to the second reach.

It all begins at the jibe mark. If you are rounding the mark with no boats within five to ten lengths behind you, you are in a great position to head right down the rhumb line. A quick look at the land behind the leeward mark will tell you if the current is pushing you one way or another. If there are boats immediately in front of you starting to go high with each other, let them go and maybe work a little lower yourself, so that when you converge, you'll be well to leeward of their wind shadows.

When you do arrive at the jibe mark with other boats nearby, try to anticipate the situation well before the mark, as it is usually a dangerous thing to be caught outside another boat. However, sometimes it's unavoidable, in which case, here are some things to remember. When boats jibe they start a new overlap for luffing purposes. So after you've both jibed, if the boat to windward of you is overlapped with you, you can luff them provided they can respond to your luff without touching the mark (rule 16.1 and 18.2(a)). In other words, you don't have to wait until you leave the two-length zone to luff, although you must be sure you have the right to luff all the boats that will be affected by your luff. So next time you are caught outside, either luff hard and try to

- If you are behind but gaining fast on a boat, be careful about overlapping them. If you overlap them close to weather, you'll force them to luff you hard, costing you a lot of wasted distance. If you overlap them close to leeward, a heads-up boat behind can take the opportunity to sail out to weather of you, as you are defenseless with your bow pinned to leeward of the boat ahead. Often, when you are rapidly catching someone, and you haven't been able to get up into the passing lane five or six lengths back, you'll have to slow down and fall in behind. This is definitely the right moment to pass on a few go-fast tips to the boat holding you back.

- Near the end of the leg, the fun really begins. If you are close behind a boat, you may be able to work them over by sailing high, forcing them up to defend, and then when returning to the mark, almost on a run, blanketing them from behind and cutting in for the overlap. Often boats will take this game to the extreme where they have to jibe to get down to the leeward mark. Usually the boat behind will try this only if they sense the boat ahead is easy pickin's. If you're ahead and someone tries this on you, tell them to "cool it," luff them good and hard to let them know you're not kidding, and whatever you do, don't let them succeed, and the word will get out that you can't be had in those situations.

FINALLY, as you approach the leeward mark, here are some moves most sailors don't execute, which will always gain you distance and often places.

- When you're coming in for your rounding, have the boat completely set up for the next beat before you enter the two-length zone. This includes having the spinnaker down and stowed, all the lines out of the water and the cunningham, outhaul, backstay, centerboard, vang, etc., all properly set. Most people wait too long and then go into hyper-panic, leaving them totally unprepared to take advantage of the critical first few hundred feet of the next beat.

- Always round the mark so that just when your sails get to close-hauled, you could reach out and touch the buoy. Never go by the buoy while you're still on a reach or a run – always close-hauled.

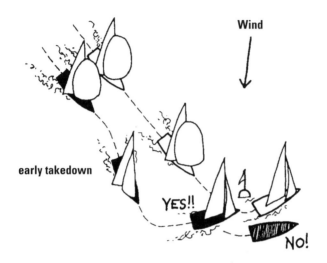

- If you are outside another boat approaching the mark, rounding on the inside means slowing down, letting them pull ahead, then rounding up on their transom. Unfortunately, sailboats don't have hydraulic disc brakes, so anticipate the situation and plan to slow down early (another good reason to take your chute down sooner).

- Also, don't round the leeward mark two feet behind the boat ahead. Give them at least half a boat-length. Often they'll make a poor rounding, be going slow, hit a wave, or have to slow down for another boat, and you'll find yourself going much faster than them with nowhere to go. You run the risk of overlapping them to leeward if you're too close, and that's the worst possible way to start off the next beat.

Going for It Downwind: The Run

A GOOD SQUARE RUN is the one time the guys behind have all the advantages. For the same reasons that it's cake for the boats ahead on the beat, the boats behind have it all their way on the run. They get the puffs and the shifts first, they have the power of suffocation with their wind shadows, and they can attack while looking forward, riding the waves, and concentrating on boatspeed.

Unfortunately, by the time many people get to the run, the Evereadys are running down, and that old killer instinct has punched out for the day. But a lot can happen on the runs if you go after it aggressively and make it happen. When you round that weather mark, get psyched to attack and grab every inch possible. Let's look at some of the ways to do it.

First, you have to know your boat. When racing downwind, there is an optimal sailing angle for every kind of boat and for every wind and wave condition. Think of racing upwind where the game is to try continually to sail as close to the wind as possible without losing speed. The same principle applies downwind, except that you want to continually sail as far away from the wind as possible, without losing speed. But because most boats don't sail optimally dead downwind, they have to jibe to get to the leeward mark. As a result, the leeward mark has two laylines just as the windward mark does.

Imagine you are hovering over the race course looking down at the run leg. A boat whose optimal downwind sailing angle is 15 degrees above dead downwind rounds the weather mark on starboard tack. The wind is due north, so dead downwind is the reciprocal, or south. The boat bears away to 195 degrees. The question is, assuming the wind and everything else stays the same, what should the leeward mark bear, so that when the boat does jibe she

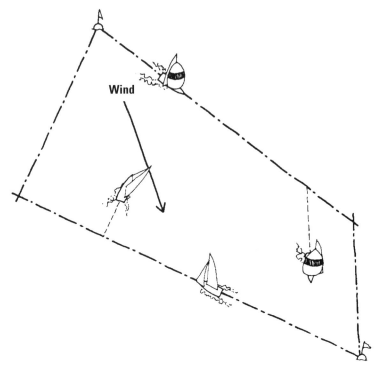

If the wind is steady, but the leeward mark is not directly downwind of the windward mark, A will have to sail longer on one tack going upwind, and longer on the opposite tack going downwind. In general, she should sail the longer tack first, both upwind and down, and never sail out to the laylines too soon.

can continue to sail her optimal downwind angle all the way to the mark? Just subtract 30 degrees (15 down to dead downwind for the jibe, and 15 up on the other side) to get 165 on port. So, when the leeward mark bears 165, she should jibe. This new course is the layline to the leeward mark. If she had jibed sooner, she would have either had to jibe back again to get to the mark or sail below her optimal downwind sailing angle, which is like tacking short of the windward mark layline and having to pinch to get up to it. If she had gone farther than the layline, she would have sailed extra distance, and though she would have had a higher reaching angle and more speed – just as when you overstand the weather mark and come footing in – the increased speed wouldn't be enough to make up for the greater distance sailed. As for strategy, the same general rule applies as upwind: don't get to the laylines too soon. Jibe early and get close to the mark before making your final approach.

Furthermore, it should be remembered that if the wind is steady and you spent three quarters of your time on starboard tack going upwind, then you can expect to spend three quarters of your time on port going back down to the leeward mark. As a general strategy it's always better to sail your longer tack first. This reduces the chance that you'll sail extra distance on the short tack, and gets you going toward the mark in case something happens down the leg (see diagram previous page).

OTHER CONSIDERATIONS for picking a favored side of the run (and for now we'll keep the wind direction steady) are similar to those for picking a favored side upwind – e.g., does one side have more wind, bigger waves to ride, better current etc.? (You should know the answers to these questions before you start the leg.) Two thoughts on current: first, the current will change your laylines; and second, if the current is flowing across the run, as a general rule it pays to go up-current first (as you'll probably be on that tack longer, it is the same principle as sailing your longer tack first).

Now, let's see how windshifts affect our race downwind. If the wind is due north, the leeward mark set perfectly due south of the windward mark, and your boat's optimal downwind sailing angle is 15 degrees above dead downwind, then on starboard tack you'll be heading 195. The question is, if the wind shifts 10 degrees to the left (backs), which way can you now alter your course to maintain your optimal 15-degree sailing angle? You're on starboard and the wind moves left, so it moves forward on your sailplan. Therefore, you can bear away 10 degrees, and instead of sailing 15 degrees above the leeward mark, you're now only 5 degrees above it. Was this shift a lift or a header? Just picture yourself going upwind: lifts allow you to sail closer to the windward mark, and downwind, headers allow you to sail closer to the leeward mark. That's why they say: upwind, tack off the headers to get on the lifts; and downwind, jibe off the lifts to get on the headers.

Now though this seems straightforward on paper, very few people seem to use this strategy on the runs. If the wind was shifting while going upwind, it's still shifting just as much going down. And if you figure that most boats lose less speed when they jibe than when they tack, logically speaking you should be jibing on the shifts at least as often downwind as you tacked on them upwind. But the problem is that it's harder to detect a small windshift going downwind than up. However, if you work at it, you can become just as sensitive. One way is to carefully watch the telltale on the shroud. Once you feel you're on your optimal downwind sailing angle, notice the angle at which your telltale is pointing. At the same time be sure that whoever is driving doesn't wander all over the place. (The compass, leeward mark, and land are all good references for steering.) Then if your course hasn't changed, and the telltale is showing the wind more aft than before, you're being lifted. Your instant reaction should be to head up and reestablish the optimal downwind sailing angle before the boat loses speed. Immediately afterward, you should jibe on this lift if at all possible.

Another excellent indicator of small windshifts is a sensitive and talented spinnaker trimmer. The spinnaker trimmer's goal is to continually try to trim the chute out from behind the main, while still keeping the optimal shape. If the boat's course doesn't change, and the trimmer reports that the chute can be trimmed more out to weather, then the wind has gone aft, and is a lift.

Another indicator of a shift is the other boats around you. If you are six boat-lengths behind another boat, sailing a parallel course, and aiming at their transoms, and one minute later you are still on parallel courses, but now you are steering a course which would bring you five boat-lengths to leeward of the boat ahead, both boats have been headed. As for positioning, boats to leeward and astern gain in headers boats to windward and ahead gain in lifts, if they jibe (see diagram).

So on the run you want to sail on the headers as much as possible. A great way to get off on the right jibe and in rhythm is to quickly resail the last beat in your mind as you approach the windward mark. How often has the wind shifted, how big have the shifts been, and is there a pattern? Then notice if you're rounding the mark in a header or a lift. If it's a lift, try to jibe as soon as tactically possible. You know you're right if you are always on the jibe taking you closer to the mark.

Now, with an understanding of windshifts, the laylines, and general geometry of the leg, let's fill up the run with other boats and see what sort of

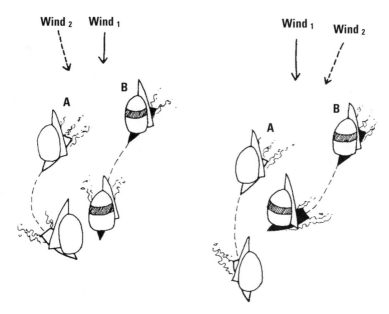

If A and B are on starboard and B is to leeward and astern of A, B will gain in a header and lose in a lift, assuming in each case that A jibes, putting the two boats on converging courses.

arsenal of tactics we have to attack and defend with. It all starts at the windward mark. If you want to go right initially, there's no problem. If there are boats directly astern you may want to head a little high for a boat-length, so as not to plant yourself in their wind shadows.

If you want to go left, it's a bit trickier. If there are a lot of boats on the starboard layline, it may be wiser to hold off on your jibe for ten lengths or so, so as not to jibe into a vacuum. If you want to go left and there are boats directly astern, be sure to bear off hard, even to the point of letting them overlap you to weather. If not, they may overlap you to leeward, securely preventing you from jibing. Also, with marks to port and all other factors near even, it pays to go on port first. You're off into clear air and water, away from the pack, and you return to the leeward mark both on starboard and on the inside.

Now, any time you want to attack another boat, position yourself so you are directly in line with their apparent wind (i.e., you should be directly in line with their masthead fly or telltales). Your shadow is effective both psychologically and realistically from as much as five to eight boat-lengths back, depending on the breeze and type of boats. If they head up to escape, head up with them; if they try to jibe away, be ready to jibe faster to get back into position. Follow your shadow down till you're right in behind them.

Now, if you are the boat ahead, check which way your telltale is streaming, then sight back in the opposite direction to see if anyone's on your air. Always sail in channels of clear air. Sometimes it's a simple matter of working up or down a bit; other times you'll have to jibe. If a boat is getting near your air, react quickly before they can get it. Often they aren't after it intentionally, and if they are and you give them a fight early on, they'll often let you go.

If marks are to be rounded to port and you are on starboard, successfully blanketing the boat ahead and about to catch them, you have to decide which side to overlap them on. If you overlap close to windward you are likely to get luffed hard. If you overlap with some distance to windward you still have to pull ahead, jibe to port, and cross them, which is very difficult. So it's best to overlap them to leeward. If you make the mark on starboard, you're on the inside, entitled to room. If you'll both have to jibe, then you can force them beyond the layline by waiting till you're securely there, jibe, and approach the leeward mark as both windward and inside boat.

If you're both on port, it's a bit trickier. If you overlap them to leeward you gain nothing – they are inside at the mark and can jibe to starboard at will. If you overlap them to windward, you'll probably get the luff of your life. The game here is to blanket them, but don't overlap them within a boat-length. This makes it nearly impossible for them to luff you. Then either they'll try to escape from your shadow by jibing, in which case you jibe so you're both on starboard and you're on the inside; or you can pull up to windward of them bow to bow on port, then jibe to starboard yourself, giving them time to respond to your new right-of-way position (rule 15). They'll most likely jibe to starboard to keep clear, giving you the controlling inside position.

If the boats are converging on opposite jibes, the boat on port should cross the stern of the boat on starboard and then jibe in for the controlling inside position. Conversely, the boat on starboard should jibe back to port before the port tacker can cross the starboard tacker's stern and get in a blanketing position to weather.

Once you are conversant with the geometry of the run, the use of windshifts, the effectiveness of wind shadows, and the fundamental boat-to-boat tactics, the run becomes a fascinating collage of opportunities. For instance, you have the simple ability to plant a boat ahead in the perfect blanketing position on a boat farther ahead by forcing the first boat up and down to escape your wind shadow. If you find yourself on the outside of a group of starboard tackers, you can quickly slow up, jibe across their transoms, and jibe back on their inside before they even have a chance to react. If you're on a lift and about to jibe, look to see if there isn't a boat ahead you can tag with your shadow on the new jibe, just to slow them up a bit or force them to jibe out of phase. And you always have the challenge to be sailing in clear air, and not to get pinned in a position where another boat is controlling you.

CHAPTER 26

The Tactical Mind

Asked if he was trying to psyche out Boris Spassky
by not showing up for the second game of the 1972
World Chess Tournament (which he went on to win
convincingly), Bobby Fischer said, "I don't believe
in psychology; I believe in good moves."

IT WAS THE LAST RACE of the 1980 Soling Olympic Trials. Robbie
Haines and his crew had already sewed up the series and had stayed ashore
to pack their boat. However, due to the boycott, the U.S. Olympic Yachting
Committee had decided to send the top two teams in each class at the Trials
to Kiel Week, which would be the last major international regatta before the
Olympics began in July. Going into the last race there were five teams – Ed
Baird, Jim Coggan, Gerard Coleman, Dave Curtis, and Peter Isler (for whom
I crewed) – separated by only 2.7 Olympic points, fighting for the valuable
second-place spot.

Basically, it boiled down to the fact that whoever came out on top would
be second overall. On the way out to the line knowing then that Robbie
Haines wasn't sailing, we figured the chances were good that one of the five
of us was going to win the race. So our strategy for the last race became winning, which to us meant playing it a little more wide open and realizing that
we would probably have to take the big chances. This thinking differed radically from our previous game plans when we just aimed for the top five each
race and accepted the fact that someone might bang a corner and win big. But
now we were dialing for dollars with five teams head-to-head on the line it
was all or nothing.

As if the anxiety weren't overbearing enough, the race committee was

forced to postpone for over an hour due to the nonexistent to barely noticeable wind strength. At first we were on our own, trying to keep our psych up
– you know, preserve that old killer instinct, depersonalize the enemy, etc.
That lasted about ten minutes. Then we sailed over to some of our friends and
tried to strike up some conversation, but everyone was feeling a bit uptight
that morning. Finally, we pulled out the old trusty frisbee, and within five
minutes just about the whole fleet was going animal for over half an hour like
a good hard-core group of junior sailors, until the race committee finally shot
the warning gun. We felt great – the adrenaline was flowing, all the uneasiness
was gone, everything was back in perspective ("remember it's just a game")
and we were totally psyched for this unique race we were about to be in.

Being Observant

As we were playing around we were also carefully noticing what was happening with the wind and weather. The breeze was east-southeast and it was
a hot, cloudless day. Puffs of two to five knots would roll through every five
to ten minutes, always more from the east. The surface water was smooth, but
there was a slight swell left over from the southwest breeze of the previous
days. There were no cumulus clouds over the land to indicate a building ther-
mal, though the forecast was for eight to 12 knots from the southwest, more
or less the prevailing strength and direction for late May in Newport, R.I. By
looking at local fishing buoys we could see that the current was flooding
(southeast to northwest flow across our course) at about half a knot. The
Stars and Tornados were already racing on their course to our east, indicating a stronger, steadier breeze only two miles in that direction.

Based on all this input, plus a tad of gut feelings, we decided to go left
initially and fight from that side of the course. As luck would have it, the committee favored the right-hand end of the line by five to eight degrees. By taking repeated wind checks we had noticed the breeze oscillating up to ten degrees, but always with the stronger puffs from the left. The line was 20 boatlengths long, so based on the math (see "Understanding Windshifts," Chapter
19) we knew that at five degrees the favored end gave a two boat-length advantage and at ten degrees, boats at the right end would have a five boat-

length jump. We also knew that in five to seven knots of breeze, a Soling takes up to 45 seconds of uninterrupted reaching to get to full speed from a standstill, that the weather end would be crowded, and that it would be very difficult to be up there and at full speed at the gun. We then figured that if we were at full speed at the unfavored end, our speed versus theirs would quickly make up for the lost distance (not to mention that we would be headed in what we felt was the right direction).

So with one minute and 45 seconds to go we sailed past the pin, heading toward the committee boat on port. We went for 55 seconds, then tacked to starboard with no one behind us (i.e., between us and the leeward end). And while most of the fleet was jamming and packing at the windward end, we reached for forty-five seconds, knowing we couldn't be early, and crossed the line full speed ahead, leeward-most boat, going for it. We knew we were gambling.

Racing Against the Fleet / Racing Against the Wind

After the start we determined that we were pretty much even with the boats to weather, but certainly not able to cross any of them if we tacked. Soon, however, we began to get headed, and one by one they began peeling off onto port. All looked "Go" for a tack, except for one slight problem: Don Cohan had gotten an excellent start, full speed right on the line, and was up on our weather hip. If we tacked, it would be close, but we couldn't cross him, and if we ducked, it would require a quick tack and a sharp turn to duck his transom, killing our speed for sure. But we did want to tack. So we cracked off a few degrees, gaining speed while we opened the windward/leeward distance between us and Don, then tacked and smoothly bore away to take his transom.

We had tacked to port for two reasons: the oscillating wind was in a left-hand phase; and the majority of the fleet, including our four foes, were heading right. At that moment most were directly to leeward, and things were pretty quiet on board *Shen*. Then the wind began going right three, then five, then eight degrees. Boats to leeward began looking better and better and some flopped back to starboard. When to tack? The fleet was splitting – Baird and

Curtis were heading left, Coggan and Coleman right. Then Coleman tacked and, watching the land behind his bow, we saw we were generally holding even, but occasionally losing ground. Baird and Curtis were crossing our transom about eight lengths astern. We could either tack then to protect our left, leaving Coleman ahead of us on our weather hip, or we could wait and get closer to see if we could make a lee-bow stick, forcing Coleman back to port and out of phase.

We decided not to commit ourselves (by tacking), but to keep our options open by continuing on port. Sure enough, as we neared Coleman we began making land on him slightly. Now for the lee-bow. As we had practiced our roll tacks and lee-bows for three months in Florida that past winter, we felt confident in our boathandling. We asked Gerard to hold his course, to let him know it would be close. He did, coming straight for us as we tacked. As our boat came to its new close-hauled course, I called "tack completed," but for an agonizing moment Coleman kept rolling over us. Pete bore off a tad for quicker acceleration, and Shen responded. Within 25 seconds we were holding even, and after 40 seconds Coleman was forced to tack away.

As the wind was now in a right-hand phase, we were looking pretty good up to weather of the gang, but our move on Coleman had allowed a portion of the fleet to get out to our left. The next backing shift left them looking good, so instead of letting them converge with us and gain we tacked well to leeward and ahead of the pack (again keeping our options open). Playing both the wind and the fleet, the rest of the beat fell nicely into place and we ended up first to the weather mark.

Staying in Control

Down the first reach we were trailed closely by Brad Alford, two lengths back, and Bruce MacLeod, about five lengths back. If either had chosen to sail high on the rhumb line we would have been forced to go up and cover, staying between them and the jibe mark. To take some control (though Brad and Bruce were still obviously free to do whatever they wanted), we communicated with them that we'd luff with them, preventing them from passing, and that by staying down on the rhumb line we'd all sail the shortest, fastest route and gain on the pack behind. They knew this was their best move anyway, and the three of us lengthened our lead on fourth place.

On the second reach we gained slightly on Brad, and as the pack was going high behind him, he began working up. We decided that we had enough speed and enough of a lead now that it would be hard for Brad to get our wind before the mark, so we stayed low, again in control, and stretched our lead over the fleet.

Around the leeward mark we stayed on port with Brad and Bruce. Ed Baird, who had moved into fourth place and was about ten lengths back around the mark, immediately tacked to starboard and we tacked with him. The wind was steadier now at about eight knots. Curtis rounded some 15 lengths back and tacked to starboard directly astern of us. Coggan and Coleman were barely in sight, though eventually they too flipped to starboard and followed us to the left, well astern. We were still in control except for one problem – Baird was going much faster than we were. MacLeod and Alford were playing the small shifts well up the right side, and we decided to let them go, and to stick with Baird. At the second weather mark it was MacLeod first, three lengths over Alford; we were two lengths back in third with Baird only five behind us now.

Anticipation... Looking into the Future

As we approached the windward mark we knew the run was going to be complex, and sure enough, all four boats did a textbook job of attacking and defending, coming into the leeward mark in a tight pack. At about eight lengths from the mark, we were on starboard just outside of Alford with Baird three lengths back. One move we could try was to jibe across Alford's transom to his inside for the overlap and room. If he jibed to defend we'd simply jibe back and would have lost very little for trying. If he didn't jibe to defend, but we didn't get the overlap, we'd still round in the same place just ahead of Baird. This was one of those many situations in which you can't lose, but you may gain, and they're always worth testing.

We quickly jibed to port, heading up across Alford's transom, bore off and jibed back to starboard to his inside. MacLeod rounded first; we were two lengths back in second, Alford was third on our transom, and Baird was fourth, on length back. Curtis had moved up and was some ten lengths behind Baird; Coggan was another six back and Coleman was deep.

Cover or Sail Your Own Race

Starting the final beat, Baird immediately tacked to starboard and we went right with him. Curtis crossed our transom and headed right, but our sights were fixed on Baird. Ed knew we would cover tightly and so, rather than go deep left with a devoted escort ready to pounce on his wind, he decided to mix it up a little, tacking early. We tried to tack to weather, giving him clear air, but he wasn't satisfied with that arrangement, and tacked back to starboard. Now, do we go immediately back with him, or reassess our race with Curtis who is working right? Tunnel vision sets in. We tack back with Baird. After a minute Baird flips again to port. He's within three lengths. This time we finish our tack to weather and slightly behind him, giving him plenty of clear air to try to nurse him back to the right. We look around. The wind is going right, and Curtis will cross us both, but Dave has to put one boat between us to beat us. We're still hanging in there, but things are getting warmer.

The wind clocks some more, and we begin to pay the price for not tacking squarely on Baird – he's faster and gaining in the header. Finally he squeezes us off and we tack. The wind clocks even more – fairly predictable pattern in Newport's late afternoons, but we've spaced it out totally. We all try to fight back to the right, but too late. The big winner is Jim Coggan who has traveled unmolested all the way to the right corner, crossing us all, and coming second overall, and within an ace of catching Bruce MacLeod for first at the line. Baird ends up third in the series with us fourth and Curtis fifth.

The tactical mind – observant, analytical, quick, careful, always asking: How did we get here?... What will probably happen next?... How will we maximize our position when it does?... Can we affect what will happen? It's the computer on board. It's also playful and clever, always trying to come up with new ways to outsmart the competition. And most of all, it hates to be beaten. Jim Coggan, wait till next time!

Helpful Tips and Racing in Current

The Little Things

More Little Things

There Is No Lee-Bow Effect

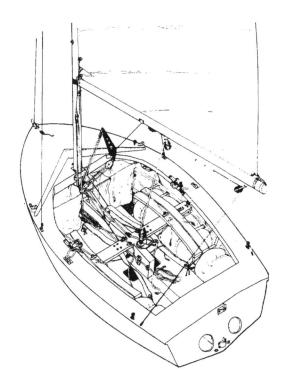

The Little Things

After winning his second consecutive
Star World Championship as Buddy Melges's
crew, Andreas Josenhans was asked what he
had learned most from Melges. His answer:
"Buddy is incredibly good at the
little things."

IT'S OBVIOUS that success in sailboat racing comes from having good boatspeed, starting well, using smart tactics upwind and down, along with avoiding the big bummers, like fouling out and capsizing. But often, the real difference between good and great sailors is their attention to the little things.

Before Racing

- Have your clothing selection worked out. Decide what the air and water temperatures are likely to be throughout the day, how wet you'll get, and how hard you'll be working. As a rule, it's better to overdress than underdress.

- Get your equipment together. Put silicone spray on all moving parts. Tape cotter pins and sharp edges to prevent serious damage. Silicone the bailers and coat the threads or inspection ports with Vaseline to insure they are watertight. Put marks on the spinnaker guys so the crew instantly knows where to cleat the guy on the sets and jibes without even looking at the chute.

- Check out the sailing instructions, particularly the recall and shorten course procedures.

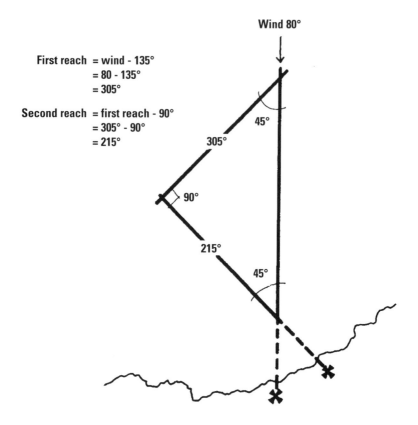

Wind 80°

First reach = wind - 135°
= 80 - 135°
= 305°

Second reach = first reach - 90°
= 305° - 90°
= 215°

45°

305°

90°

215°

45°

45°

- Do your compass course headings homework (diagram). If the marks are set before the race starts, take land sights for the different legs (diagram). To do this, sail from the leeward mark toward the jibe mark and take a bearing. Then return on the reciprocal bearing. As you head back toward the leeward mark, look beyond the mark for a land reference that lines up with you and the buoy. Write it down so you don't forget it.

On the Starting Line

- Get a Line Sight (more on this in Chapter 13). If you're using a boat anchored off the leeward end as your sight, be sure they're official and will stay put. If they are official and sighting the line through the pin, watch the direction in which they're looking to determine where the other end is.

- Get right up to the committee boat to actually hear the countdown for the warning gun. Shapes and sound signals are often vague and unsynchronized.

- Stay outside or above the line as long as possible to take wind readings. Also, notice your reaching angle as you sail down the line. This is an excellent last-minute check, as a different reaching angle than before indicates that the wind has shifted.

- After a general recall, immediately watch to see if the committee moves one end or the other, as this will change your land sights, and possibly your strategy. Note where the good sailors, and particularly the good local sailors, started.

- In an adverse current (i.e., current setting you back behind the line), sail back and forth above the line or, in clear air at the ends. But never sail below the line, especially in light air. Avoid starting near the leeward end. When the current is pushing the fleet over the line, stay clear of the windward end.

- Avoid jibing before the start. It takes you away from the line, and is a much riskier maneuver.

On Windward Legs

- In waves "pick the path of least resistance through the water."

- When feeling slow, ease the sails – "When in doubt, let them out."

- When you're moving well, keep the boat flat.

- When tacking, look to windward and ahead about one boatlength, making sure you have smooth water to tack into.

- There are often different wave angles on different tacks; set your boat up to go best, even if it means readjusting after each tack.

- When two close-hauled boats are converging from a distance, it's critical to know who's ahead, particularly if you're on port. Watch the land off the starboard tacker's bow. If more and more land is appearing to windward of him, you are "making land" on him and will cross, and vice versa.

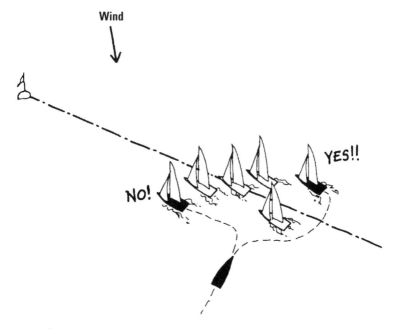

- If you decide you want a port tacker to cross ahead of you, don't yell, "Go ahead!" "Go" sounds too much like "no," and usually, the guy will lee-bow you instead. Say "Cross" or "You can make it." But the best means of communication is for you or your crew to actually catch the eye of someone in the other boat and give him a big wave. This is particularly important in international events.

- If you do decide to duck a boat, be sure to ease your sails and keep the boat trim perfect throughout the maneuver. Too often, people bear away with their sails trimmed in tight and wind up losing the starboard tack advantage on the return crossing.

At Marks

- When nearing the starboard tack layline, don't tack onto starboard to leeward of another starboard tacker, unless you are sure you will make the mark (diagram). After about fifth place in a crowded fleet, the wind and water is extremely disturbed, and it's always better to be on the safe side in getting around the windward mark.

- Around the weather mark, especially going onto the first reach, don't be in a hurry to set the spinnaker. Come around, check out the situation, know where the next mark is, go a little high with lots of speed and the jib eased, board up, cunningham off, etc. Then set and come blasting over people.

- In large or tightly packed fleets, don't tack immediately onto starboard after rounding the leeward mark. There'll usually be too much traffic, bad air, and disturbed water from the second reach and end of the run.

- At the leeward mark, your chute should be down and the boat complete-ly set up for the next beat (outhaul, cunningham, vang, etc.) by the two boatlength circle. Don't spend the first 100 yards of the next beat tidy-ing up with your head in the bilge. It's much more important to be sail-ing fast and getting on the right tack.

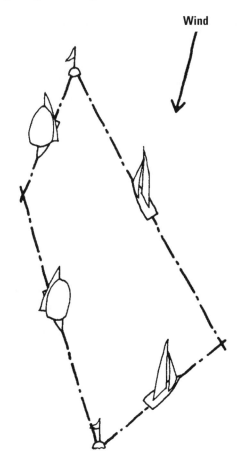

Wind

Starting the Run

- At the end of the beat preceding the run, determine whether you just spent more time on port tack or starboard. The opposite will be true on the run (diagram previous page).

- Determine what phase the wind is in as you approach the mark. If you approached the mark in a huge port-tack lift, set onto the starboard jibe for the first part of the run.

- If there is current moving across the course, consider taking the jibe heading you up current of the leeward mark. That way, you'll eliminate sailing extra distance in the end. When you can see the mark, watch the land behind it. You'll then know exactly which way the current is moving you, if at all.

- All else being equal, it is tactically better to jibe to port initially, as this will give you the inside and starboard advantage coming into the leeward mark. Just be careful of close-hauled boats still on the beat, especially when you are setting the chute, for they will all have rights over you.

Wind

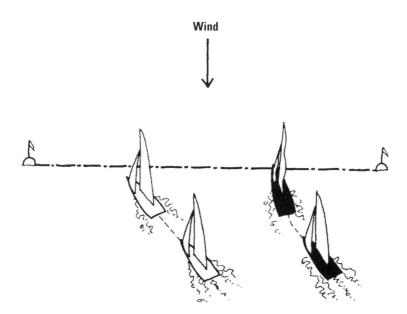

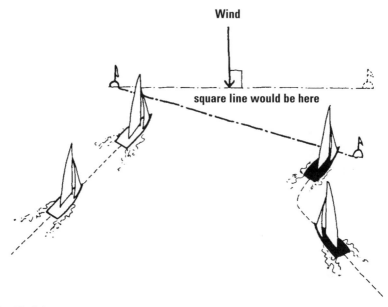

Wind

square line would be here

At the Finish

- Always finish at an end. If the line is not square and you finish in the middle, you've sailed extra distance. If the line is square and you're finishing in the middle, you are at a disadvantage in a close situation, as you aren't as sure when to shoot head to wind. And in all close finishes, shoot the boat perpendicular to the line with a full head of steam (diagram previous page).

- If your start/finish line is in the middle of the beat and the wind is steady, the end that was not favored at the start will be favored at the finish, i.e., the more downwind end (diagram).

Little Things in General

- Telltales made of magnetic tape, such as cassette tape stick less to sails and shrouds when wet than traditional yarn.

- Immediately after a capsize, the first person to the bottom of the boat should kick or bang the bailers shut. The sharp edges can be dangerous.

- Keep the boat dry throughout the race.

- Check the area for weeds. In a keel boat, be sure to back down before each start. In a centerboarder, pull the board completely up at each mark before checking the rudder.

• Know what equipment and sails your competitor is using so you can relate boatspeed and trim.

Most important, look around all the time. Look for flags on marks and boats in the vicinity and up the course. Often, the race committee flag is your best indication of how to approach the finish line. Watch the sky and the clouds and head for those big black ones. Check out the lobster pots for local current information. Remember, if you're fumbling for the hiking straps, fighting with the spinnaker halyard, or simply lost as to where the mark is, you're not racing – you're just sailing around.

More Little Things

THE SPORT of sailboat racing is pretty complex, and it can often seem that the better you get, the more elusive the top becomes. One reason is that the top guys have a whole repertoire of subtle little things they do, in all areas of the sport, to give themselves an advantage on the course. So here are more little things in which I'll continue to reveal some of the less obvious, but often race-determining little things that happen aboard the winning boats.

Starting

- Avoid jibing before a start. In light air it can take you farther from the line than you think, and in a breeze it's too easy to dump or break a boom, or take on water.

- Most boats with a main and jib slow faster by luffing the jib rather than the main. To stay high in a hole on the starting line, overtrim the

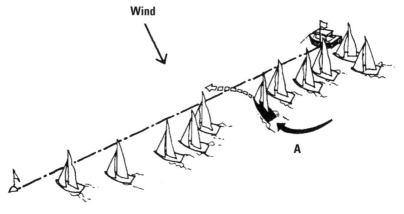

Boat A sails into the upper edge of a hole between two boats and stays high by luffing the jib and overtrimming the main. Shortly before the gun, A bears off, trimming the jib and easing the main for speed.

main and luff the jib. To accelerate, trim the jib and ease the main (diagram previous page).

- Get land sights through both ends of the starting line.

- Practice two or three timed runs at the line. Use the watch and your land sights to be at an exact place at an exact time, preferably the place you plan to start. This gives you a great feel for how the wind is shifting and the effect of the current, as well as giving you faith in your line sights and practice in accelerating and slowing.

- Tape one stopwatch to the mast or some highly visible place, so everyone knows the time and can see it at a glance.

Rigging

- Sew your batten pockets closed, especially when it's windy.

- Telltales tied to shrouds and backstays have that disturbing way of wrapping themselves into oblivion. Buy or make a light plastic bushing which is held at the right height by wrapping tape around the shroud. Then attach the telltale to the rotating ring.

- For a masthead wind indicator, I prefer the rotating arrow variety with sighting arms, such as the Windex model, rather than a flag or other type. Set the arms for your average jibing angles downwind, not your tacking angle up wind, so that when the arrow is between the arms downwind you know immediately that you're heading too low and going slow.

- Mastbend reference marks on the main are very useful. First lay the main out flat on the floor and find a point about halfway up the luff of the sail. Measuring aft from this point, mark three or four vertical lines at two-inch intervals. Then when sailing, if you're sighting from the gooseneck to the tip of the mast and your line of sight goes through the third line aft, you know your mast has six inches of bend (diagram next page).

- Put large numbered marks by your jib leads, traveler car, mast partner (for noting fore-and-aft position of mast), etc. For wire controls like

the backstay or vang, twist the wire open and put in short pieces of whipping thread or marlin every two to three inches at a section of the wire that enters the deck or sheave. Keep a notebook record of the adjustments and in which wind and water conditions they were fast and slow.

- Carry a scoop-type bailer like a sawed-off Clorox bottle and tie it in with the end of a halyard tail.

- Try to get a universal hiking-stick attachment that allows the stick to swivel in any and all directions. Be sure your stick is long enough to allow you to put the helm all the way to leeward when you are fully hiked to windward. If it isn't, make it longer. Ski pole shafts make excellent hiking sticks, and most ski shops have a pile of poles with broken tips, etc., which they'd love to give you.

- Using Magic Marker or a tight, one-inch whip on the line, mark your guys to the exact place they'll sit in the cleat when the pole is as far for-

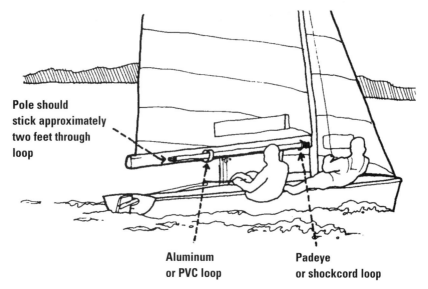

Pole should stick approximately two feet through loop

Aluminum or PVC loop

Padeye or shockcord loop

ward as you'll ever carry it (so you can find the mark without taking your eyes off the chute). Then in a wild heavy-air jibe, you can luff the sheet and cleat the guy in the correct place while the pole is being wrestled back onto the mast.

- When financially possible, use low-stretch line, such as Spectra or Kevlar etc. for all spinnaker sheets.

- Clearly mark the spinnaker halyard so you know instantly if the chute is all the way up.

- A fast way to set the chute is to have the skipper hoist the halyard. Lead the halyard aft, through a strong cam cleat mounted near the aft section of the centerboard trunk and back through a small bullet block on the keelson by the skipper. The cleat should be raised so that when the halyard is tensioned it pops into the cleat automatically. To release the halyard, grab the line between the block and cleat. Because most leeward marks are left to port, mount the cleat on the port side of the trunk for easy release.

- After checking the class rules to be sure it's legal, strongly consider storing your spinnaker pole on the boom. We've used it with great success on the Soling and Lightning. The advantages are quick launching and storage, no longer having it under foot and, most important, never again wedged into the skipper's face – all of which far outweigh any possible disadvantages, such as added windage. In designing a storage system, avoid open hooks, which can catch lines and rip spinnakers. Instead, attach a large loop on the outboard end of the boom using a ring cut from PVC or one made from pliable aluminum. For the inboard end (near the gooseneck) rivet a padeye on either side to clip the pole into, or tie a shock cord loop around the boom to slip the pole through (diagram previous page).

- When it's time to drop the chute, the halyard must run free. If the tail is stowed by the mast, feed the halyard into its bucket, starting with the tail. If the coils are left on deck, be sure the tail is kept about two feet away from the coils to prevent accidental knots. On the Soling we used to throw our halyard tail overboard coming into the leeward mark. Not only did it never foul, but the slight friction of the water kept the chute from dropping too fast. However, be sure to toss the tail to your buoy rounding side, i.e. if you're turning to port, throw the tail to port. Otherwise, you might end up the way we did once, with the tail securely wrapped around the rudder post!

- Put a large mesh screen over your bailer so tails of line, bits of disintegrated circulars, leaves, etc. can't plug up the works.

- The top guys in each class are probably most in tune with the latest in rigging ideas for that class. At a convenient time for both of you, ask them to share their thinking on the various systems. Possibly they'll have time to look at your boat and can suggest the easiest and least expensive ways to improve some of your rigging. Be aggressive about your learning.

Clothing

- Over the past five years a surge of attention has been given to the clothing one-design sailors wear. Wearing the right clothing does make you sail faster. You can buy any of this gear from a number of good businesses that advertise nationally in sailing magazines.

- One-piece foul weather suits are lighter, more comfortable, and less expensive than the traditional two-piece foul weather suits. Also, in many cases, they are warmer, longer lasting, and drier.

- Hiking boots. The old sneaks are great for kicking around in, but when it comes time to jump in the straps, your ankles and arches will love you forever if you buy a pair of sailing hiking boots.

- Full-fingered gloves. The traditional sailing gloves with all five fingers cut off can cause more pain than wearing no gloves at all. The stubby fingers slip down and bunch at the bottom, and nothing protects the critical outside of your fourth and fifth fingers, which do all the work. Full-fingered gloves with maybe just the thumb and forefinger cut off are the most comfortable.

- And for those cold, wet days, there's no substitute for a wool hat, wool socks, and drysuit or wetsuit. The wetsuit should be the Farmer John style (one-piece, long legs, no sleeves).

Preparation on the Water

- Start the race with no water in the bilge or tanks. The crew should keep the boat bailed and sponged dry up to the last possible second.

- If you're using the automatic bailers, close them for the final minute while you're luffing before the start, and open them again just as you begin to accelerate.

- Sailing around before the start, keep a slight heel so waves can't wash over your windward side as easily.

- Check all double-ended controls. If the first reach will be a windy, tight one on starboard, be sure to have plenty of excess tail on your starboard vang, traveler, and cunningham controls.

- Put all your loose things (tool bags, lunch, sail bags, foul weather gear, etc.) into one large sail bag and tie it into the boat.

- Carry plenty of short pieces of spare line, basic tools, a knife, a few shackles, some spare battens, and anything else you feel you may need.

- In a keelboat carry a weed stick. A long ski pole with a towel wrapped at one end works well. Just put it in the water ahead of your keel and the force of the water will push it down the leading edge.

There Is No Lee-Bow Effect

ONE OF THE MOST fascinating and timeless controversies in our sport is over what effect current has on how we sail and race our boats. Beginning in early 1979, Peter Isler and I filled hours of time debating the effects of current, and it wasn't until mid-1980 that he finally parted my clouds and shook me loose from years of misconceptions and incorrect assumptions. Here then is my understanding of the effects of current, substantiated by several of my more mathematically-clever friends.

What Is Current?

Current is the physical movement of the water. Often the entire body of water moves, as in a river or tidal region, but frequently just the surface layer of water moves, as when swept by the wind.

How Can We Determine the Current?

The information we need is: in what direction and at what speed will the current be moving at a given location and time? In tidal regions, tide charts tell us the times and height of low and high tide, but they don't give us specific information on current. In the fourth hour of a six-hour cycle, how fast is the current moving? Nearing low tide, when does the current actually start flooding (coming in)? After high tide, where does the ebb (going out) begin? Many regions have current charts and tables. Ask the locals or at the nearby marine store. The current is further affected by high and low atmospheric pressure, the phase of the moon, the strength and duration of the wind, the topography of the bottom, and the amount of rainfall or snow run-off in the area.

With over 30 feet of snow in the mountains north of San Francisco Bay the winter of 1982, local sailors reported that the currents were much stronger and less predictable that summer.

After studying the charts and tables and talking to the locals, go out and take your own measurements. The best current stick is one that protrudes only a couple of inches above the water's surface (to reduce the effect of the wind), and sinks to the level of your centerboard or keel. A weighted plastic tube works well, but in the clutch a sponge does the trick. Drop it in next to a buoy and start your watch. When it has drifted a boat-length, check the time and direction it moved. Using r = d/t, you will know the strength and direction of the current.

Check the current all over your racing area. Bring a small buoy if there aren't many already out there. If you're measuring current several days in advance of a regatta, remember that the current cycle often changes. Using your tables, determine the predicted direction and strength for your race day. Then find what time that same direction and strength occurs the day you're going out, measure it at that time, and check your findings against the table. Also observe all lobster pots, buoys, and anchored boats for clues on current. Finally, notice the water's surface. When the current is aligned with the wind, the water will appear extra smooth; when opposing the wind, the water will appear rough and choppy.

How Does the Current Affect Our Apparent Wind?

This is the most difficult aspect to conceptualize, but once understood it solves the mysteries surrounding current. As Peter says, imagine a stick floating down a river. Whether it's angled parallel or perpendicular to the direction of the current, it is still being moved at the same speed and direction down the river. If you go out on the river on a floating boat when there's no wind, and the current is from the south at two knots, what will the boat feel? Two knots of wind from the north.

Now the true wind picks up to ten knots and you look at your instruments. The wind direction and strength they read will be the combination of the two knots of current created wind and the ten knots of true wind. The

Effects of Current on Apparent Wind

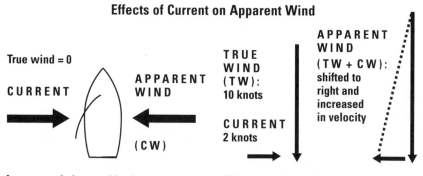

True wind = 0

CURRENT

APPARENT WIND

(CW)

TRUE WIND (TW): 10 knots

CURRENT 2 knots

APPARENT WIND (TW + CW): shifted to right and increased in velocity

Apparent wind caused by the current moving the boat through the air **(CURRENT WIND)**

This new wind is the direction and velocity in which the boats will race.

This chart shows changes in apparent wind angle and velocity (as noted) due to different angles of current (black arrows). The true wind is 10 knots from the north (000°). The current strength is 2 knots. As an example, if the current was from the east (the three o'clock position) the resulting apparent wind (true wind plus current wind) would be from a direction of 349° at a strength of 10.2 knots.

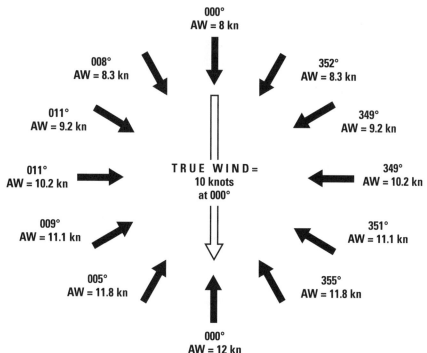

000°
AW = 8 kn

008°
AW = 8.3 kn

352°
AW = 8.3 kn

011°
AW = 9.2 kn

349°
AW = 9.2 kn

011°
AW = 10.2 kn

TRUE WIND = 10 knots at 000°

349°
AW = 10.2 kn

009°
AW = 11.1 kn

351°
AW = 11.1 kn

005°
AW = 11.8 kn

355°
AW = 11.8 kn

000°
AW = 12 kn

result is one wind direction and strength (true plus current wind) in which you will sail. Now you put up your sails and begin sailing. The apparent wind your boat now feels is the combination of the true plus current wind and the headwind your boat is creating by its forward motion. It's important to remember here that no matter how fast or in which direction you are moving, the current speed and direction remain constant (assuming the current itself doesn't change), and therefore its effect on the boat's apparent wind will always be present and constant (diagram previous page).

Should the Current Affect the Way We Sail Our Boats?

Assuming that we're sailing in constant current direction and strength, NO! As we've determined, the direction and strength of the current created wind is the same no matter at what angle the boat is aiming or at what speed it is moving. The presumption of the lee-bow effect is that if you are sailing directly into the current you can pinch slightly, putting the current on your leeward bow, and the current will push you up to weather. This is obviously false because the only direction the current can move you is in the direction it is going (the stick on the river).

The presumption of those who believe that in current a boat will have a different apparent wind direction and strength on opposite tacks, is that on one tack the boat will be slowed more by the current than on the other. The extreme example is when port tack takes you right into the current, and starboard tack takes you across it. The illusion is that on port tack it would seem that the boat is still going forward toward the wind, but that on starboard the boat is being swept away from the wind by the current. Therefore, the apparent winds must be different on the two tacks. The fallacy here, though, is that the judgment of going toward the wind and being swept away are made in reference to fixed objects such as the mark, an anchored boat, or land. In reality, both boats are being affected equally by the current and the wind "sees" both boats in the same way. In other words, if you were following the race in a motorboat and were in the ocean where you couldn't see any land for reference, the boats would look identical on either tack, and in fact you would have no clue that there even was current unless you knew from charts or perhaps from the surface condition of the water. Put another way, if you're sailing on a boat with apparent wind strength and direction instruments, they'll read the same on both tacks because the boat is affected in the same way by the current on either tacks (the stick in the river again). Stan Honey's numerical model and Dave Dellenbaugh's geometric model, found at the end of this chapter, are both proofs of this phenomenon, and they look at the two boats both from the reference frame of the water (i.e. as the wind "sees" the boats, or as you would floating in another boat) and from the reference frame of land (i.e. watching from the bottom, an anchored boat, or on shore).

How Does the Current Affect Our Racing Strategy and Tactics?

The current has a definite effect on our race around the buoys (because the buoys are fixed to the bottom), and in some places, like Charleston, S.C. or San Francisco Bay, the current is often more of a race-determining factor than windshifts. Race committees must remember to determine the wind direction before anchoring. Often they'll anchor and then take wind readings, which of course will not determine the wind direction and strength in which the sailboats are sailing. Using the diagram showing the effects of current on apparent wind for reference, if the RC anchors in one knot of southerly current, then sets the starting line perpendicular to the true wind which is west, which end is favored? The right-hand end, because the new true plus current wind is shifted right. Fortunately, because our sailboats are not anchored, when we shoot the wind the current's effect is automatically built in, so we see only one wind direction (true plus current wind). So in current, don't determine the favored end by judging the angle of the flags on the line.

Before the start, especially in light air, always stay on the up current side of the line. Never allow yourself to get down current unless absolutely necessary. This often requires paddling or motoring until your preparatory signal to get up current. Also, get excellent line sights through both ends of the line. (Go outside one end, sight through both ends, and see what shore object lines up with the starting marks.) In current, always watch the land behind fixed objects to see how you're drifting. To arrive at a mark you cannot aim at the mark. Instead, aim up or down until the land stays constant behind the mark.

On the start put all faith in your line sight, and sail in whatever direction and speed keeps you lined up. You'll be amazed at how useful the land sight is.

If the current is pushing you downwind away from the line, avoid the left-hand end completely! Set up earlier on starboard and remember that the more you slow down, the farther you'll be set from the line. Stay up there using your line sights. If the current is flushing the fleet over the line, stay away from the right-hand end. Practice timed runs to get a feeling for how far to hang back and when to break for the line. In current pushing you from left to right, again avoid the right-hand end, and consider a port tack approach, especially if the left end is at all favored. And in right to left current, the left end is a devil's trap. Plan a middle to right end start.

Once you've started you will undoubtedly have a game plan based on all your info on the wind, the different currents over the course, and your tactics for the race. If you know you are in bad current headed for better current, you might consider footing slightly to get out of the adverse current faster. Likewise you might pinch a bit to stay in favorable current longer.

But no matter what the current is, it will change your laylines to the windward mark. In general, try to take the up current tack first, i.e. in a left to right current across the course, go on starboard tack first. This minimizes the risk of overstanding. Near the mark, plan to tack onto starboard well short of the mark and go to the port tack layline, again to insure against overstanding. Finally, if you're close to making the mark on starboard, you can often pinch, slowing the boat and allowing the current more time to move you the little bit needed to the right relative to the mark.

For more accuracy in determining laylines in current, Brad Dellenbaugh has a good idea. Before the start, pass right next to a buoy going close-hauled on starboard and sail for a minute. Then take a bearing back to the mark and write down its reciprocal. Then, assuming similar current at the windward mark, when the mark bears your number, you'll be on the layline.

On the reaches (and at all marks) immediately locate the mark and watch the land behind it. When the land holds constant behind it, you are sailing on the shortest possible course to it. If you expect the current to set you more to leeward ahead, be sure to work extra high early, etc. On the run again in general, sail the up current tack first. Using Brad's method (sailing by the buoy on your optimum downwind angle before the start) will help you call the lay-lines. Also, with the current at all aft, those marks come flying up to you, so start your spinnaker take-down and mark rounding preparation early. Finally, when rounding marks in current watch the land behind the mark. The tendency is to watch only the mark, which will always result in a less than ideal "swing wide-cut close" type of rounding.

RACING IN CURRENT adds a great new dimension to sailing. Do your homework so you know what the direction and strength of the current will be throughout the race. Remember, for optimum speed through the water, you should not sail your boat any differently just because you are in current; but also keep in mind that the current will definitely affect your tactics, especially in regard to lay-lines, rhumb lines, marks, and your strategy when the current varies in different places on the course.

NUMERICAL MODEL *by Stan Honey*
GEOMETRIC MODEL *by Dave Dellenbaugh*

Assumptions:

1. True wind with respect to land blows from 000° at 5 knots. (AZ)
2. Current flows from 030° at 1 knot. (AB)
3. Boats tack through 73.79° and sail at 2 knots. (This angle is chosen so that the port tack boat, sailing in the combined true wind/current wind, is headed directly into the current.)

In Reference Plane of Water:

Wind (ref. water) = Wind (ref. ground) (AZ) plus Water (ref. ground)
Wind (ref. water) = 000° at 5 knots plus 030° at 1 knot (AB)
Wind (ref. water) = 353.10° at 4.16 knots (BZ)

This is now the wind in the reference plane of the water. The boats symmetrically tack about this heading; they head 030° on port tack (ZK) and 316.21° on starboard tack (ZC). *Diagram 1 (next page)*

Both boats are moving through the water at the same speed: 2 knots. Since both boats (port and starboard) sail the same angle with the wind

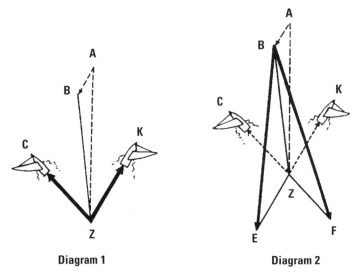

Diagram 1   **Diagram 2**

(ref. water), and both boats sail at the same speed through the water, then by simple trigonometry, both tacks have exactly the same apparent wind: 5.89 knots (BE on port, BF on starboard). *Diagram 2*

In Reference Plane of Land:

Port-tack boat

Movement (ref. land) = Movement (ref. water) plus current (ref. land)

Movement (ref. land) = 030° at 2 knots (ZK) minus 030° at 1 knot (JK)

Movement (ref. land) = 030° at 1 knot (ZJ)

Apparent wind = Boat movement (ref. land) plus true wind (ref. land)

Apparent wind = 030° at 1 knot (ZH) plus 000° at 5 knots (AZ)

Apparent wind = 004.87° at 5.89 knots (AH)

Starboard-tack boat

Movement (ref. land) = Movement (ref. water) plus current (ref. land)

Movement (ref. land) = 316.21° at 2 knots (ZC) minus 030° at 1 knot (CD)

Movement (ref. land) = 287.05° at 1.97 knots (ZD)

Apparent wind = Boat movement (ref. land) plus true wind (ref. land)

Apparent wind = 287.05° at 1.97 knots (ZG) plus 000° at 5 knots (AZ)

Apparent wind = 341.36° at 5.89 knots (AG)

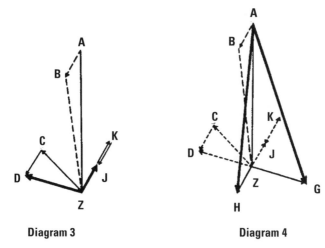

Diagram 3   **Diagram 4**

Notice that the port tack boat is slower over the bottom and at a closer angle to the wind, but the strength and direction of the apparent wind felt on each boat is still exactly the same. *Diagrams 3 and 4*

Psychology in Racing

CHAPTER 30

Inner Sailing

"Think of your competitors only as
a guide to your own performance."
– Paul Elvström, International
and Olympic champion

(After a poor first beat.) "Well we're here...
just for fun, let's see how well we can
do in the rest of the race."
– The late Manton Scott,
Sears, Intercollegiate, and 470 champion

"It's difficult to have fun or achieve concentration
when your ego is engaged in some heavy ulterior
game involving its self-image."
– Timothy W. Gallwey,
author of The Inner Game of Tennis

TO MOST WHO ARE BENT ON IMPROVING their racing skills, on
the surface these quotes offer very little substantive information. In reality,
however, these words are rich with insight into how to successfully approach
the game of racing sailboats. I'd like to try to expose what, to me, is much of
the meaning of these statements. This will be most meaningful to those seriously interested in improving their enjoyment and success in racing and who
will expend the energy to consider carefully what is being said, look inside
themselves for a possibly renewed understanding of themselves and, if necessary, rearrange some of their priorities and attitudes.

I'm often asked which books on sailing have been most useful to me. The one book that has had the most profound effect on my finishing positions and my attitude toward the sport is Tim Gallwey's *The Inner Game of Tennis* (Random House, N.Y.). Gallwey writes: "Every game is composed of two parts, an outer game and an inner game. The outer game is played against an external opponent to overcome external obstacles, and to reach an external goal. Mastering this game is the subject of many books offering instructions on how to achieve the best results. But for some reason most of us find these instructions easier to remember than to execute."

"It is the thesis of this book that neither mastery nor satisfaction can be found in the playing of any game without giving some attention to the relatively neglected skills of the inner game. This is the game that takes place in the mind of the player, and it is played against such obstacles as lapses in concentration, nervousness, self-doubt and self-condemnation. In short, it is played to overcome all habits of mind which inhibit excellence in performance."

AS I TRAVEL around the country teaching racing seminars to all ages and levels of sailors, I'm continually impressed by how much knowledge and experience people have, and how seriously people take their racing. It's fantastic. Why then don't more of these people win races more of the time? Why do some people's learning curves level out and never seem to rise again? Why do people complacently fall into established "pecking orders" within their club series? And why the frustration, the anger and the inability of some people to get along in a boat?

Even at the highest levels of our sport, where all the top competitors are sharp both physically and mentally, it fascinates me to see how some consistently emerge as even better than the best, particularly under the pressures of a nationals, worlds, or Olympic Selection Trial. Certainly they possess skills, whether consciously or subconsciously, that would be helpful to all of us to learn. So, with the guidance of Gallwey's *The Inner Game of Tennis*, let's explore the inner skills, and try to learn how to use them.

Sailing Out of Your Mind

Think back to your last successful race or series, and try to remember how you felt during the competition. Most people's descriptions include the following: "I felt good"; "I felt relaxed"; "Things seemed to go my way"; "It seemed too easy." All these descriptions imply effortlessness and almost surprise at the outcome. Athletes in most sports use similar phrases, and the best of them know that their peak performances never come when they are thinking about them. In fact they seem to come when they are "out of their minds."

In this state the good sailors are not unconscious of what is happening around them, but in fact are more aware and concentrated on the speed of the boat, the subtle changes in the strength and direction of the wind, and the tactics. They aren't aware of giving themselves lots of instructions – tack on the headers, stay with the fleet, pick the path of least resistance through the waves – they just do it. They are conscious, but not thinking, not overtrying. They seem to be immersed in a flow of action which requires their energy, yet results in greater speed and accuracy. The "hot streak" usually continues until they start thinking about it and try to maintain it. As soon as they attempt to exercise control, they lose it. Consider the classic scene of a sailor or team jumping out to an early lead in a series and then sailing poorly only to lose in the end. The question then is: how do we become "out of our minds" without thinking about it?

The Discovery of Two Selves

Gallwey outlines a convention to help us better understand what happens within us. He divides us into two selves: Self 1 and Self 2. Self 2 is the computer, the unconscious, automatic doer. Self 1 if the teller, the director, the worrier. The kind of relationship that exists between Self 1 and Self 2 is the prime factor in determining one's ability to translate knowledge of technique into effective action.

Decide for yourself the value of this typical scene: You're coming onto the jibe mark, it's blowing 25, and you're in first place. You've successfully jibed hundreds of times before so that Self 2 knows exactly how to do it. All of a sudden Self 1 gets into the act, as if he doesn't trust Self 2 to do it right. "Now this is important; we can't afford to blow it here. Be sure to turn quickly, but bring the boat back under the boom. Okay., here we go. Careful, careful... CRASH!" By thinking too much and trying too hard, Self 1 has produced tension in the body. Furthermore he heaps the blame on Self 2 – "You stupid &#!£@! Of all the times to blow it. Can't you get your act together?"

In hindsight, if someone had told Self 1 (your mind) to do nothing during the jibe but concentrate on the water directly in front of the bow, you probably would have jibed perfectly, and you probably would have caught the first wave after the jibe, gaining several lengths in the process. So sailing "out of your mind" is really just a matter of shutting Self 1 up so that Self 2 is allowed to perform in its excellent way.

Getting It Together

Getting it together means Self 1 is totally supportive of Self 2 and does everything possible to help Self 2 perform up to its potential, which in most people is nearly limitless. When the two are in harmony, one's peak performances can be reached. When Self 1, the ego mind, is constantly chattering away, constantly thinking, and constantly deriding Self 2, Self 1 does nothing but interfere with the natural doing process of Self 2, causing frustration and poor performances. The most important skill Self 1 can learn is to become an objective rather than a judgmental observer of events. See events simply as they are; don't judge them as good or bad. It's when emotions are added to events that people begin to get overconfident or start to freak out, both of which seriously inhibit clear decision-making and performance.

A classic example of this occurred when I was crewing for Bill Shore in a Lightning class championship. It was the morning of the first race and we were unpacking his boat, which had just been shipped home from Switzerland. As I peeled the cover back, I saw that the entire deck surrounding the mast partner had been crushed. Reluctantly I told him, expecting him to be extremely upset and disappointed that we couldn't sail. Instead he looked at it, grabbed a paddle, wedged it in for support, taped it all together and started unpacking the rest of the boat! Instantly, I realized the value of remaining calm, detached, and objective in the midst of rapid and unsettling changes.

The spinnaker halyard jams, you're expecting a header but start to get lifted, a boat totally in the wrong smashes into you, the mark is in the wrong place, you have a bad race – all these things are events which you may have not expected and which may even cost you places in the race or series. But they've happened; there's nothing you can do about it. Given the chance to think about the situation as good or bad, the emotional Self 1 will start to bum out, give up, and the situation will get worse. But the player of the Inner Game will remain calm because his judgmental mind is quiet, allowing Self 2 to spontaneously and accurately figure out the best way to make the most of the situation and do its best from that point on.

Concentration – the Here and Now

The key to an undistracted mind, hence the key to the Inner Game, is relaxed concentration. Concentration is the act of focusing one's attention. As the mind is allowed to focus on a single object, it stills. As the mind is kept in the present, it becomes calm. Concentration means keeping the mind here and now.

You come off the line immediately to windward of a fast guy. You get nervous that he'll blow you off. He does. While cursing the fact you started there, you tack. Your mind's in the past. The boat to windward of you tacks simultaneously right on your air. In anger and frustration you shove the tiller over again, cursing out your crew for not being ready. Going slow and in bad air you resign yourself to a bad finish, taking the opportunity to call yourself a loser and consider selling the boat. Your mind's worrying about a future outcome. Your head is blown, your race is blown, and you're everywhere but in the present.

The art of keeping in the present is a difficult skill which must be respected and practiced hard. Remember, the outcome is only the sum total of all the mini-events leading up to it. Focus your energy on successfully completing each mini-event – the pre-race preparation, the start, the first five minutes of the race. Don't ever let your mind consider the importance of the outcome. As Ben Franklin put it, "Watch the pennies, and the dollars will take care of themselves."

If you feel your mind drifting away from the present, gently bring it back, giving it something of interest to focus on. In the Laser, when I'm tiring and my concentration begins to drift, I get near another boat or watch the waves off my bow, trying to actually see if the water moves up or down the face and the backside. There's no question that when the mind is in the present, focused exclusively on what's happening right there and then, things seem to happen slower, decisions are more spontaneous and accurate, and the body has more energy.

The Meaning of Competition

Why do we race sailboats? Out of sheer love for sailing, for the enjoyment of competing, or as an extension of our ego needs to excel at something, to feel like a winner? In our achievement oriented culture one thing comes through loud and clear: excellence is valued in all things, and a man is measured by his competence in various endeavors. That is, you are a good person and worthy of respect only if you do things successfully.

In this light it's frightening to realize that people use sailboat racing, with all its inherent fickleness, uncertainties and inequities, as a standard for judging self-worth. Notice your own attitude as you go to school or work Monday morning after winning or not winning on the weekend. On the one hand you may feel happy, confident, on top of the world; on the other, depressed, lacking confidence, and feeling that you'll never succeed in anything. But you are exactly the same person you were on Friday; you've just let the outcome of the race dominate your outlook on yourself.

The fundamental skill that underlies all others of the Inner Game is the ability to see winning for what it is: overcoming obstacles to reach a goal, which might be making it around the course, finishing five places higher in a series, or winning an Olympic Medal. Often, reaching the goal itself may not be as valuable as the experience that can come by making a supreme effort to overcome the obstacles involved. Thus the competition can be more rewarding than the victory itself, though it takes a certain level of maturity to see this.

The player of the Inner Game is in a moment-to-moment effort to let distractions go and stay centered in the here and now, where his total energy goes toward doing his best. As he proceeds around the race course, his competitors become merely guides to his own performance. And his satisfaction and happiness come in the end when he knows that he performed well against challenging obstacles. As an added bonus, the successful players of the Inner Game will find they are enjoying the sport much more, and walking off with more than their share of the silver.

CHAPTER 31

The "If Only" Blues

"If a frog had wings, it wouldn't spend all
its time hopping around on the ground."
– Overheard at a party of Tufts sailors

HOW MANY TIMES have you been struck down by the "if only" blues?
You shoot the finish line to miss winning by a boat-length; you wind up a series
in fourth, but only a narrow three points out of first; you tie for third overall in
your district, where three teams go to the nationals and you lose on a tie-break-
er. All of a sudden, the blues hit you – first in the stomach with that sort of
sickening feeling you get when a pocketful of cash gets shredded in the wash-
ing machine. Then the blues swell up into your throat and finally land in the
brain, right in the frustration center, leaving even the best crying, "Man, what
a drag. If only…"

As for myself, I could fill a songbook of blues from my past. "If only we
had sailed our own last beat, rather than trying to cover three boats in the
last race of the Olympic Trials, we could have qualified for Kiel Week… If I
hadn't gone for the leeward-end of the starting line, I wouldn't have capsized
rerounding it… If we hadn't measured in just our heavy air sails at the Soling
Worlds, we would have done much better."

Even worse are the pure and simple mistakes that could have been easily
avoided with a little more care and forethought. For instance: "If I hadn't uncleated the jib by mistake at the start of the last race of the Lightning South-
ern Circuit, we would have won in Miami… If I hadn't capsized twice at the
Pan-American Trials, I could have qualified for the U.S. Team… If only my
traveler line hadn't broken at the Laser Worlds, I wouldn't have had to stop halfway through the race to fix it." Nothing will harm you more than thinking

you could have done better if only you had done something different. But when it's all said and done, the only thing that goes into the history books is the final score. So, knowing how miserable it can feel, I'd like to propose some cures to ridding yourself of the "if only" blues.

It's true that sailboat races are lost, not won, and that the competitors who make the fewest mistakes will wind up on top. But you can't just keep on racing year after year and expect the mistakes to go away on their own. The game is too complex, and improving at it just doesn't come that easily. And I see so many people who love racing and have invested tremendous amounts of money, time, and energy in the sport, making the same mistakes over and over. If racing well means something to you, be smart and do it right. Don't be passive about your learning – get psyched and attack it actively.

THE MOST COSTLY TROUBLE on the race course can be traced to one of seven big bummers:

- being over the starting line early
- being caught in the fourth row at the start, when the fleet is only two rows deep
- not quite making the windward mark in a crowd
- hitting a mark
- fouling another boat
- capsizing
- having something on your boat break

As we've all heard so much about these devil's traps on the course, it's easy to take them for granted and not think about them. But at least one of these seven will always lie behind a DNF, DSQ, or an unnecessary 15th on the scorecard. However, all of these are things over which we have total control. At the root of 99 percent of our mistakes are carelessness and greed. So, next time you race, concentrate hard on not being careless or greedy and you'll carry an inward smile from ear to ear as you watch some other guy trying to reround the jibe mark with his spinnaker still up.

Once you've eliminated these completely from your repertoire of ways to lose the race, there is a longer list of slightly smaller bummers (although bummers, nonetheless) waiting for you along the race course. They include:

- not knowing the course (especially when leading the race)
- not knowing the current
- shooting a corner on the first beat
- being trapped outside of other boats at the jibe and leeward mark
- overstanding the windward mark
- bad boathandling, resulting from never having practiced other than in a race

Again, these are careless mistakes and not the kind of things you'd like to admit to after the race is over; yet they are extremely costly to your finishing position and cause tremendous frustration among everyone involved.

THERE ARE SEVERAL WAYS to overcome these needless pitfalls and to put it all together. And they all begin with the premise that you want to improve your racing ability and that you realize it will take energy and work to do so. A person's learning curve is plateau-like; it rises sharply until the person stops trying, then it levels out. Once renewed effort is applied, the curve rises again. The common occurrence is for people to try hard to improve, see themselves getting better, and then sit back and say, "Hey, I'm getting to be pretty good." At that point, they usually let up, expecting their improvement to keep climbing. But it won't. In fact, it may even slip back a bit, causing them some frustration, and perhaps even causing them to doubt the same techniques that got them there in the first place. At any rate, their learning cycle will level out. Thus, you have people who have been racing for years who just don't seem to get any better and those who've just recently started who are improving like gangbusters. It's all a matter of attitude, and it is directly proportional to the amount of effort you put into it.

The first step is to identify your strengths and weaknesses, examining which mistakes you seem to continually make. Grab a notebook and get together with the people you sail with. List all things you do well on the course and all areas you feel are holding you back. Then, think back on the last few regattas you attended and list as many of the mistakes you made as you can remember. Keep these on separate pages.

From then on, after every race or series you sail, add or subtract from these lists. If, realizing you were weak on spinnaker work, you went out and practiced a couple of evenings and now you're blowing them away on the sets, change spinnaker sets from the weak list to the strength list and briefly jot down how you accomplished the change. If you can think of other mistakes you made, add them to the mistake list. Also jot down wind and sea conditions of each race so you can not only see what mistakes you made, but in what conditions they occurred. If you don't have time to write all of this information down, try using a cassette tape recorder, making your lists as you drive home from the regatta, while everything is still fresh and everyone's talking about it anyway.

Once you have a good feeling for what most of your mistakes are, here are some ideas on how to reduce them. With so much to continually think about in a race, it's impossible to remember it all, so make lists of areas you have the most trouble remembering and write them on your boat. For example, though I've had very little Star boat crewing experience, I was invited to sail in the 1980 Star World Championship, where it blew a steady 15-to-18 knots for the entire series. Coming into the leeward mark, on a screaming plane with other Stars close by, it was all I could do to think about getting the jib in and hiking, much less trying to remember to retighten the upper and lower backstay, put on the cunningham and outhaul, readjust the jib cloth tension, move the jib leads back inboard, open the automatic bailers, reset the ram, stow the pole under my hiking straps, and slacken the forestay. Quickly realizing this after a disastrous leeward mark rounding in the practice race, I thought out all the things that had to happen at the rounding and what seemed to be the optimal order in which to do them. Then I wrote the entire list on the deck by the mast, and we never had a problem after that.

Indeed, there is absolutely nothing wrong about writing messages to yourself on your boat. On their booms, various people have written "Compass," "Check In," "Weeds," (on the port side) "Ease main when ducking starboard tackers" and "Flat is fast." Around compasses you'll see "Port header higher," reminding that as the numbers read higher on port tack, they are getting headed. Around the boat you'll find messages like, "Stay with the fleet and grind," or "More starboard upwind, more port down." A great Finn sailor who had blazing speed but hit a lot of corners wrote the simple question, "Tacked recently?" These messages are very helpful and result in less energy spent trying to remember them and more spent doing them right.

BEFORE THE START, there's a tremendous amount of research and preparation to be done, and a list can help you avoid the mistake of not doing it all. The list should include:

- spinnaker hooked up properly
- tanks bailed dry, everything tied in
- sails set properly for first beat (check others' sails)
- favored end, line sight, current
- what the wind's doing
- watch wind
- foils clear of weeds

All of these lists and comments can be worked out ahead of time in your notebook and, after races, the lists should be augmented or changed as better ways are found.

ONCE ON THE COURSE, your state of mind is very important in minimizing the number of mistakes you make. Mike Loeb, winner of the 1980 U.S. Olympic Trials in FDs, sums up three very important attributes to success in his CCA rule: concentration, common sense and anticipation. Even when you know all the mistakes not to make, it takes thinking about them continually not to make them. It's when your mind gets distracted by something else that trouble strikes.

Keeping your concentration up through an entire race takes a lot of energy on your part. Every time you feel your mind slipping away from thinking about what's happening and what mistakes you could make next, you have to push it back. External distractions, such as an unmotivated crew, or internal distractions, such as fear of heavy air, detract tremendously from your depth of concentration and result in many more mistakes.

Common sense is another critical area. It very rarely pays to take an unnecessary chance in sailing, yet people do it all the time. Sticking your bow in for an overlap when it's very close to the two-length zone, trying to cross a close port tacker, or going for the leeward end start usually all wind up in disaster. Given a choice of several alternatives in a situation, let your common sense be your guide. Don't take chances unless you're 100 percent sure you'll get away with it. Unnecessary greed is the cause of most big mistakes.

And finally, anticipation – the ability to think ahead to what's going to happen next – is crucial to avoiding your own mistakes and taking advantage of other people's mistakes. You know that as you approach a windward mark on port a big mistake will be to end up to leeward of the starboard tack layline, forcing you to tack back to port to lay the mark. Yet, again, people do it all the time. As you come into the mark, look ahead and imagine what's going to happen. If there are starboard tackers close to the layline, tack on their lee-bows only if you are sure you can make the mark. It's always better to duck a few transoms and get around the mark safely. Often, there will be a slight header, an accumulation of bad air, or a little extra windswept current, and the guys whose transoms you ducked won't make the mark themselves. By being conservative and anticipating the trouble, you'll round the mark safely and possibly pick up a few boats in the process.

As you sail down the reaches and runs, think back on the previous beats and determine a strategy for the next one. Based on what you know and have seen, try to anticipate what's going to happen on the next beat. It's always better to have a plan that goes wrong than to have no plan at all, as then you

can analyze your mistakes and correct them for the future. Remember, in theory, there's always a reason for everything that happens.

If you go into a situation with other boats and come out on the short end of the stick, immediately (then or shortly after the race) resail the incident in your mind and discuss it with the people involved. Try to figure out why you lost out and what you should do differently the next time you encounter the same situation. Your goal should be to get to the point where, if you don't do well, at least you'll be able to know why and identify the mistakes you made.

There's nothing more frustrating than to do poorly and know that you've made some big mistakes. Yet, very few people go beyond feeling bad to eliminating their mistakes in the future. Whether you're skipper or crew, take the time to write down all the mistakes you make in a race, and while racing, try hard to concentrate on eliminating your mistakes by continually asking yourself, "What's going to happen next?" and by avoiding carelessness and greed. It's almost impossible to completely eliminate the "if only" blues, but then again, there's no better feeling than when you put it all together and win.

CHAPTER 32

Crewing for Paul Elvström

IN SEPTEMBER 1982 Brad Dellenbaugh (my teammate in our Soling campaign) and I had the opportunity to crew for Paul Elvström in the Yacht Racing/Cruising Hall of Fame Regatta and I thought I'd try to share that experience, because it's not the sort of thing that happens every day.

In early July I confirmed that we'd be sailing with Paul and from then on the regatta was a bright spot on my calendar. As much as I was fascinated with the fact that I was about to be sailing in the same boat with someone who had been almost a storybook legend for as long as I could remember, I was even more curious to see if the way Paul sailed was any different than the styles of the other excellent sailors I'd had the chance to compete with and against over the last few years. And interestingly enough, it was.

The most striking difference was that when it was time to go sailing, man, we went sailing, and there was never a wasted moment. No sooner had we jumped off the launch than the sails were coming out of the bags, and Paul was right up there to help put them on. When he was putting the jib snaps on, they went on in a hurry. When the battens were going in, they hardly saw the light of day before they were snug in their pocket. As soon as the halyard shackle was closed, up went the sail – and splash, we were off the mooring and headed out. If it was downwind sailing out, the chute was up fast; upwind, and the boat was set up for speed, and we were sailing as fast as possible so Paul could check our speed, make any adjustments, get the feel of the boat, and get to the racing area as quickly as possible.

The concept of not wasting time and doing things that would directly increase our chances of doing well in the race was an undercurrent that ran through everything we did; it was present, almost instinctively, in everything

Paul did personally both on the water and off. If he was in our way where we were rolling the chute between races, he'd almost leap to the other side, and when he landed it would be a soft, graceful landing. If we were going upwind to check the sails before the start, he'd trim the mainsheet as fast as possible, not only to get going upwind sooner, but also to rehearse the action in case he had to trim the mainsheet around a mark. This characteristic of being continually driven to optimize every situation he was in came very naturally, and yet the sustained level of its intensity is something I haven't seen in a sailor before.

The regatta was sailed in Etchells-22s, a boat Paul had never been in before, and the first race we sailed was the practice race, with Jud Smith filling in for Brad. Jud had been sailing in E-22s in Marblehead, Mass., for years, and Brad and I had just finished a week sailing with an excellent E-22 sailor in the Worlds, so, going upwind before the start Paul let Jud and me set the boat up as best we could, and then he gave his own comments. He was very easy to give input to, and yet he was always checking things out himself and making small adjustments to see how they worked. Of course Jud and I were electric, trying to meet Paul's level of optimization and give him as much information on the local conditions and what was going on as we could.

BEFORE THE START we did all the usual things such as checking the wind, getting numbers on both tacks, checking the starting line, getting a line sight, etc. After a nice start in the middle of the line we were going upwind, and Jud and noticed that the first beat was very short due to the lateness in the afternoon of the practice race. Our position was good for a two-mile beat, but in this sprint there was no way we were going to be able to move out and cross the half dozen boats to weather of us before arriving at the port tack layline. So we gave Paul the scenario and, after a quick look we tacked and ducked the six or seven starboard tack boats that had been to weather. Consistent with everything else he did, when Paul ducked he ducked perfectly, keeping full speed close-hauled until the starboard tacker was about a boat-length away, then bearing off to a reach, aiming for a point about three feet up the starboard tacker's leeward side, then cutting within inches of the boat's stern and heading back up to close-hauled as our stern crossed their wake.

Anticipating a crowd at the first mark we overstood slightly and rounded close behind about five or six boats.

As the course was a windward-leeward, twice around, we set immediately, and Paul chose to bear off on a course to leeward of the group ahead. Sailing by the lee for almost a minute, Paul was in effect pinning the starboard tackers to windward from jibing, and at the same time he was carefully watching for boats astern. As soon as one was about to cross our stern and blanket us, we jibed onto port in clear air and to the inside of the first six boats. Next thing I knew we had pulled out slightly ahead of the others, and I took my eyes off the chute momentarily and noticed that we were laying the leeward mark!

Sailing down the run, Paul felt he had too much lee helm and had both Jud and me sit to leeward, whereas almost everyone else had both the skipper and chute trimmer on the windward side. Also, he had me playing the guy farther forward than I'm accustomed to, and though I usually let the luff of the chute curl over momentarily every few seconds, he felt I was "letting too much pressure escape" and had me trim it tighter. Of course this took more concentration not to overtrim it, and again I felt myself digging in and trying even harder to raise myself to the high level of perfection Paul was continually after.

Having controlled the inside, we arrived at the leeward mark first, and Jud and I were psyched for that "perfect" takedown and rounding. Having thought through everything before we arrived, the chute came down like a dream, and as Paul steered us perfectly around the buoy, Jud and I trimmed the jib and main in unison. The high feeling of satisfaction was so strong that as we shot away from the mess astern, Jud and I couldn't hold back a "Nice sailing, Paul!!" And with a smile he said quietly, "Like the old days."

"Like the old days…" Every time I stopped to think about whom I was sailing with during the weekend, I just got this huge inner grin. I mean this guy had won two Olympic gold medals before I was born; two more before I was in my first race. But over the course of the weekend the only awareness of Paul's huge success in sailing came from everyone around him. After about the hundredth person had come up and taken his picture, Paul looked at us and said, "What have I done?"

If you didn't know his history you'd never learn it from him unless you asked. He's much more talkative about what's happening in sailing right now – the popular designs, the trends in the rules and tactics, the new wave of boardsailing, and changes that can help the sport in the future, etc. When we weren't racing, Paul was very low-keyed, had a good sense of humor, and we discussed things from politics to the America's Cup to his family and what they were up to.

But when it came to racing, he was 100 percent serious about it; his attitude seemed to be, "I don't mind if I'm not winning, but if I'm not trying my hardest to race as well as I can, it's not fun... and when I'm racing well and all the other people around me are racing well also, then that's when sailing is really fun." And when Paul gives 100 percent, the atmosphere in the boat becomes very alive.

For one, he's an absolute perfectionist, so that every maneuver has to be done as well as possible. Also, before and during a race he's extremely sensitive to all the clues around him, constantly looking for as much information as possible about the wind, current, what the course is, and what people in the other boats are up to (previous to the first race we had gone through the list of sailors, and he had made mental notes of which ones were likely to be tough).

During the race there was always talk, and if we got quiet he'd ask for input: what the compass read, how our speed and pointing were, where the other people were, where the mark was, etc. Throughout this he was concentrating intensely on steering the boat and was continually moving Brad and me around to balance his helm. As for tactics and position, he would look at a situation, review our input, and then make his decision. He's probably seen almost every situation before, but still I was impressed at how rarely we were doing something that didn't seem right. Coming into crowded marks we always wound up on the inside, and we always seemed to have good speed coming out of the marks.

Only in one race did things go badly, and Paul showed a bit of temper that you knew had to exist with his level of intensity. After rounding the first mark of the fourth race in third, we were going down the run, and the committee had moved the leeward mark to the right (looking upwind) in response to a large left-hand shift. Brad and I both looked downwind and saw a mark that was on a broad-reach course in front of us and another mark farther to leeward more in the direction of the posted compass course of the new mark, which was on the nearby race committee boat. Assuming the lower mark was the new leeward mark, we told Paul this and as the fleet began to go high above us, Paul decided to work low away from them. About halfway down the leg Brad and I both realized that we had made a mistake and that the new leeward mark was the one that had been previously in front of us. Bumming heavily, I told Paul. About six or seven boats had already gone over us to weather, and it was obvious we had lost big. Paul was understandably upset and let fly a few words in Danish which we didn't need a translator to get the drift of. But then, almost instantly, he said, "Well, okay, never mind," and settled down and began concentrating on our new situation. In fact, for the rest of the race (in which we were battling for tenth or worse) Paul never showed any frustration except for an occasional "This is not fun" as someone would tack on us and force us to go the wrong way. But inside I knew how he must have been feeling.

SAILING WITH PAUL will always be one of my most special experiences in the sport. I, like thousands of other racers in the world I'm sure, have always had tremendous respect not only for his unparalleled racing accomplishments, but also the contribution he's made to the sport with his work on the racing rules, tactics, sailmaking, yacht designs, hardware, clothing, coaching, and the rest. But having spent three days racing with him, I can see clearly how he came by his many highs and occasional deep lows in the sport. He's not only very observant, but also a good listener who hears what people are saying around him so he has as much information as is available when it comes time to make a decision. He also loves sailing and has tons of energy when he's doing something he believes in. But the key to Paul is that he's a perfectionist, not an egotist. He wants to do things well, not for himself, but because otherwise they're not worth doing. And he has an intense inner drive that demands perfection in everything he does, which continually shows both on and of the water.

In reflection, being with Paul for those three days was tremendously helpful in my own Olympic campaign, because in examining my own intensity and drive for perfection, and then comparing it to his, I saw that I had a long way to go. And he made real to me what I've always known and heard myself teach, but which I've never felt so strongly: the key to winning and succeeding is not only to enjoy sailing thoroughly and to study and know all the things necessary both to prepare for racing and to race well; but almost more important, to actually do every little thing that you know you should do and not to be satisfied until each one is done perfectly.

CHAPTER 33

Are We All Playing the Same Game?

*"You haven't won the race, if in winning the race you've
lost the respect of your competition" – Paul Elvström*

IN MY BOOK *Understanding the Racing Rules of Sailing*, I've tried hard
to explain the racing rules as they're written in the rule book. Consider for a
second what the rules are for: they tell us what we can and can't do. Driving
rules tell us we have to come to a complete stop at stop signs, that we can't drive
faster than the speed limit, and that we can't drive when we're drunk. Why
were these rules written? Because people saw that cars could hurt and kill them
and others, and they saw the need to create a system in which people were
safe, in which they'd know what to do and expect in every situation. Why
don't people always stay within these rules? Because the rules restrict them,
they hold them back. People feel in control of themselves – they aren't going
to hurt anyone, and they don't need a bunch of rules to tell them what to do.
Unfortunately what they don't see or care about is that this attitude is conta-
gious ("Hell, he's going 60, why should I poke along at 35?") and that their
peer pressure is pretty strong ("C'mon, we haven't had that much to drink,
let's hit the road").

It's easy to see that this attitude of not caring about the rules is what poi-
sons a system and makes it dangerous and unpleasant for others. To change
the situation, the people affected call for enforcement, of which there are two
kind available: external and internal. In driving, the external enforcement is
the police, the unmarked cars, the speed traps and the threat of paying money
for tickets or losing your license, etc. Internal enforcement comes from many

places. Maybe we've been involved in an accident or seen one where people have been hurt or killed, and our fear or our concern becomes strong enough to make us want to stay within the rules' limits.

In the world of sailing, where we're dealing with many different kinds of people, the stakes of winning are often high: business, money, prestige, our self-image and ego, acceptance, etc. And when we lose (i.e. don't win the regatta) we feel bad or frustrated or angry not simply because we didn't win, but because we won't get all the things that come along with winning. And what's worse, we can't avoid watching as the winners rake it in.

So we have a game going here with winners and losers, and we have a network of rules that form the system in which we play. The rules for sailing are *The Racing Rules of Sailing*, the rules of the class being raced, the rules for the regatta (i.e. the sailing instructions), and a fourth set of rules – the "human" rules. The last are the rules that govern our behavior more than anything else, that say when we decide to enter a game we agree to play within the rules and will give our best shot to overcoming the obstacles and challenges to winning; but they also say we'll respect the people we're racing against and won't pull any cheap shots in order to beat them.

While I was watching a post-game show after the Super Bowl, I heard a pro linebacker say, "One thing that the team which won does so beautifully is that their ends run a series of 'picks' on the defensive backs, which is basically illegal, but they're so smooth that they rarely get called for it. That's how they get people open so often." It's easy to see that they'll have more completions, more passing yardage and more points scored, etc., all of which reflect highly on the quarterback and the coach (who obviously know what's going on). But until the issue can be brought out in the open, documented, and proved, hardly anyone seems to notice; and while the quarterback and coach are tanning themselves in the rays of their success, other teams are already plotting similar plays for next season.

To some people who sail, this is the real world. They're in it for themselves, for the attention, the publicity, the lime-light, and the business. Of course they're going to do everything possible to try to win. Why not? Isn't that what it's all about? So what if they cut a mark at night, knowingly race a boat that was measured in illegally, or lie in the protest room. "Big deal!"

they say. "It's just a race. C'mon, I'll buy you a beer, I just have to talk to these reporters first…"

To others, this attitude seems pretty shallow. Sure, they want to win too, but to them there are some parameters within which the game must be played. They love it when they can tack right in front of someone with only a few feet to spare because they know the other person will hold his course until the tack is completed, and then immediately head up and keep clear; or when they're on port and cross someone on starboard by inches, and nothing comes out of the starboard boat except "Nice sailing." They'd do the same thing too. They want the other people to be racing at their best, because that's when it's the most challenging to try to win, and the most satisfying when they do. Their question is, "How can it feel good to win when you know you've somehow cheated the people you've beaten?"

It's almost as if the game can be divided into two categories of players. One is the group that, to varying degrees, will intentionally go outside the limits of the rules (including the "human" rules) to try to win, feeling that as long as they don't get caught or get thrown out on a protest, they've done nothing wrong. The other group is the people who see racing as a personal challenge, a series of obstacles including the other competitors, the boat, the physical demands, the organization of a campaign, etc., all of which must be overcome to emerge on top. It would be meaningless to them if it were easy, and it would deflate the whole challenge to go outside the rules to win.

When you stop to think about it, these two groups are, in fact, playing two entirely different kinds of games and this is the bottom line of a lot of the trouble in sailing. How then do we reconcile these two groups on the same race course? One side calls for more enforcement; the other denies the whole problem on the surface, with the attitude: "C'mon, get with it; stop being Joe Righteous. Let's have some fun." I sense that this division in attitude and conscience is the cause of many of the hot issues that we debate in sailing today, such as professionalism, means of propulsion (rule 42), and gross breach of conduct (rule 69).

Let's look at the pumping, rocking, ooching scene (rule 42), and more specifically rocking, which is the most common illegal action. Again, there are two elements: the rule and the enforcement. The rule is clear in that it specifically defines what rocking is, and then prohibits it at all times. It's fair to say that most sailors know when they are intentionally rocking their boat or when they are deliberately letting the boat rock even though their bodies aren't moving. In both cases the boat is rocking and the rule prohibits that.

NOW FOR ENFORCEMENT. The problem begins when someone in your fleet makes the conscious decision that he or she doesn't care what the rule says, and is going to go faster by rocking. Now he's gaining an advantage over you, so you have to make a decision; either do nothing, try to stop him, or start rocking yourself. If you're confident that the system of enforcement is there to back you up, you might yell to the guy to stop it, and if he doesn't, then protest. But if you sense that the protest is going to cause a lot of tense feelings (no one likes to be the bad guy) or that it will probably be disallowed anyway, you'll either sit there and get upset, or join in. The upset feeling gets even worse when you feel people are doing it all over the course and that by throwing one guy out, you're not really solving the problem.

This unsettling atmosphere is leading sailors to call for more judges on the race course to police rule 42 actively (external enforcement). But it's not that they actually want judges on the course; they just want to be confident the everyone is playing the game the same way so that no one has an unfair advantage and the racing remains a good challenge. It would be no fun racing your Pinto against a Ferrari, just as it's no fun sailing by the rule while people rock by.

The truth is that we sailors don't trust each other to enforce the rules internally and it's right here, at this lack of trust for each other, that we have to start to work. For a fleet, or class, or group of us assembled at a regatta, the first thing to see is that we need everyone to want to come out and race: otherwise there'd be no regatta. Also that the racing is the most fun for everyone and the most challenging for the top guys when we all agree to leave the B.S. on short, and go out and race hard within the rules.

This attitude will work only if everyone agrees with it, and the best way is to have a meeting of all the sailors and bring it out in the open before the racing begins. A few simple words such as: "Hey, we all know all the sleazy moves and we know what's going on, and it will be a lot more fun if we just leave that stuff ashore," get the message out. Also, there may be specific problems: people not doing Two-Turn Penalties, too many general recalls because people just aren't holding back, or rules that people aren't sure of or have different interpretations of, and it's very important that these be discussed ahead of time. Even if the group's idea of pumping isn't the same as another group's somewhere else, at least everyone will know how the game's being played in the upcoming racing, including the judges and race committee, who are the external enforcers of our game. This is critical.

ANOTHER ELEMENT that greatly increases internal rule enforcement is rules knowledge. To this end, we should open the doors to our protest hearings. Let the people who have never been in the room before see how the rules work. This can also serve to cut down on the bogus protests. Many protests involve at least one person who knows he is wrong but feels that he may be able to win the protest on a technicality, or by his presentation to the committee. This is morally wrong, and it will be a lot tougher to do this with all his peers peering at him. Of course there would be some necessary ground rules such as: 1) total silence; 2) once in the room no one leaves until dismissed; 3) named witnesses remain outside; and 4) disturbance is grounds for some sort of penalty, etc.

To me, the real meat and subtle nuances of the rules are discussed in the "deliberation" segment, and that's the segment in which people would really learn a lot. Also, opening this up would help the committees remain more objective and base their decision solely on the rules in the book and the facts as they came out in the hearing, rather than on suppositions and personal prejudices. Short of this and time permitting, the committee should at least allow the audience back in for the verdict, and explain how and why they made their decision. This is especially important at youth events, but should be applied across the board.

Also, US SAILING has a pool of certified judges and has appointed a regional administrative judge (RAJ) in each region of the U.S. These people can be very helpful in locating qualified judges for your regattas, giving rules talks, and helping interested people to become better judges. Their contact information is available on the US SAILING website (www.ussailing.org) under

"Racing / Race Administration."

It all boils down to: "What game are we playing out there?" For those who have actively raced for a couple of years, what's really going on around them and what the tricks of the trade are is no mystery. So it's really a matter of making the inner decision of what we are and aren't going to do. I'd like to propose that though it's tougher to win when we stay within all the rules – including the one that makes us morally responsible to our friends to sail fairly – the best racing is when we can trust each other to play it straight, respect each other to try our hardest, and see ourselves improving from the challenge. No external system of enforcement will ever be as effective as our own internal agreements to all play the same game. Unfortunately, it takes only one person to burst the bubble.

Talk about this with the people you race with.

Safety

Safety and
the Racing Sailor

Safety and the Racing Sailor

AT A SOLING REGATTA outside this country I was suddenly and dramatically made aware of the underrated importance of safety in one-design racing. It was a rough, windy day, but the conditions were certainly the kind in which most fleets would start a race. The wind was a steady 22-to-25 knots with waves from four-to-six feet, which caused the waves to be very steep and close together. There were nine boats in the race.

It was the fourth race of the regatta. We were second in the series and were psyched for the heavy air, feeling we had a chance to win the race. We took the start and were a close second at the first mark. Down the reaches we slipped back a bit, but we were pressing hard up the second beat. Halfway up the beat I noticed that we were accumulating a lot of water in the bilge. When one of my crew checked, he found that several of the control lines were out through the bailer, restricting the flow of water, and couldn't be pulled back in because the ends were knotted. We also discovered that the reason why the bailers appeared to be working on the first beat was that most of the water had been draining through cracks in the false bottom into the free air space below. Now, with that space full, the water was filling up the bilge, and with the bailers sitting low in the water and clogged, and the boat going progressively slower, the water was draining less and less. Another boat passed us right at the weather mark.

As we rounded the mark and started the run, I decided to set our small spinnaker, figuring that our increased speed would bail the boat faster and that it might be our last chance to pass the two boats ahead, neither of which had set their chutes. We sailed for about a minute, got everything ready, and then went for it. Our system called for the middle crew to hoist the chute as fast as possible, for the forward crew to hold the pole forward and tend the sheet, and for the skipper to pull the guy back. Everything was going fine until I momentarily looked up to oversee the operation and clear the guy. That's when the boat suddenly started down a wave.

All the bilge water rushed forward, the boat instantly submarined, and when I looked at our bow, it was a good two feet under water and going down. I quickly jammed the tiller to leeward, popping the bow out. Now our cockpit was half filled with water. My crew got the chute down remarkably fast, but the boat was becoming very unmanageable. At one point we rounded up, the boom hit the water, immediately laying the boat over, and for a few seconds I was standing with one foot on the keel. With the pressure off the sail, the boat sprang back up, but now the cockpit was about three-quarters filled.

I had never encountered such a situation and had never thought through what I would do if it occurred, so I had no immediate plan of action I could fall back on. I knew we had to get the main down immediately, but as long as we were reaching, the pressure was too great on the halyard lock to release it. So I waited until I was at the crest of a wave and then quickly spun the boat into the wind, trying to keep the boom from digging into the water to leeward. We made it head-to-wind, but I knew we would have only a few short seconds to release the main before the boat was blown back onto a reach and knocked over again.

When I ran forward to help my crew get the main down, I discovered three problems. First, my forward crew had been having trouble keeping his life jacket on due to a faulty zipper, and had tossed it up under the foredeck before the start. Now he was unable to find it. Second, the line for the cunningham control had been a bit short, so we had to put tension on the luff to get the cunningham hook in. Now it was a time-consuming operation to remove the hook to release the strain on the luff so we could get the main down. Finally, I found that the main halyard tail had come uncoiled and had tangled itself in everything imaginable – and none of us had a knife to cut the rope free from the wire.

Just about this time, the stern started to sink slowly below the surface. I quickly scrambled up to the bow with one of my crew, while the other held to the mast. We floated like this for almost a minute. Then I heard the water rushing into the forward bulkhead, and the boat began to sink from under us. One crew and I gradually worked our way up the forestay with waves crashing hard over us. Knowing that our greatest danger was getting swept away from the boat, we held tightly to the rigging. Finally, just as we all arrived at the top of the mast, the boat touched bottom. About five minutes later we were picked up by the rescue boat. If it hadn't been for the shallow water, the three of us, one without a life jacket, would have been floating free in the water for a dangerously long period of time.

The whole incident was a sobering experience, but it was nothing compared to the shock of learning that, at almost the exact moment our boat had gone down, another Soling had sunk at the other end of the course. I don't think I'll ever forget the horror I felt when told, "Two men rescued, one man dead."

The other boat had abandoned the race at the end of the first triangle, having taken on a lot of water on the reaches. Sailing a close reach toward the harbor entrance, the skipper realized that he was still taking on too much water, so he decided to take down his main and run to a secondary harbor entrance about a quarter of a mile downwind. By now they had been out of the race for about ten minutes. They had detached their hiking gear from the floor of the boat, and a rescue launch was keeping an eye on them waiting to take them in tow when they got into the calm water of the harbor.

They were only a minute away from the entrance to the harbor when a wave lifted the stern, the water in the boat rushed forward, the bow submarined, and the boat began to sink. The three crew members swam free and were holding onto the stays of the slowly sinking mast, waiting for the rescue boat to pick them up. Suddenly, in the surge of the waves, the hook on the hiking harness of an 18-year-old crewman hooked itself around the forestay between two of the jib snaps used to hank the jib on. He was momentarily pulled under one of the waves and, whether he swallowed too much water to think clearly or simply froze in panic, he didn't immediately unhook himself. As the boat slowly pulled him down, the other crew went to help, but by then the boy was totally panicked and kept grabbing desperately at his friend. Unable to free the boy, his friend finally had to surface.

This incredible tragedy took place so fast in what seemed to be a situation under control, that even now it's hard to believe that it could have happened. How do such things happen? It's easy to say that the boats were at fault or the sailing area was too dangerous or that the sailors were too inexperienced. But this wasn't the case. The sailors were experienced and familiar with the waters. There was no sudden squall, nor were there cold, blustery winds. It was a warm, windy day, beautiful for racing. And the Soling is an extremely safe boat with an outstanding safety record since its introduction in 1967.

Instead, the basic problem was in not respecting the fact that such a tragedy could happen and thus not knowing what to expect and how to react. For my part, it never entered my mind that a boat I was sailing could sink. I've raced numerous keelboats, including Shields, E-22s, J/24s, Atlantics, and a full Olympic campaign in Solings. I love heavy air and have had some of my best finishes in the most extreme conditions. And in all my years of sailing, I have never been in a situation that could be considered even remotely dangerous. I've always been physically and mentally prepared for heavy air, and I've always made sure my boat and equipment were ready for racing in it. In short, my overconfidence prevented me from even thinking that I could sink a boat.

In retrospect, I'm not at all proud that the boat I was driving sank. But I'm not so ashamed that I can't tell you exactly what caused the accident, what mistakes we made throughout, and the many things we could have done differently to avoid the experience altogether. My first mistake was that when I spent time going over my borrowed boat to make certain that it was ready to race, I ignored some non-performance oriented problems. Almost all the boats in the fleet were ten years old and had been built without false bottoms, which instead were installed by the sailors over the years. The boat I was to race had not been sailed in for over a year and had several small cracks along the edge of the false bottom. There was only one medium-size bailer on each side, as opposed to the one large and one medium that are more frequently used. The two bulkhead hatch covers were held on by shockcord rather than the mandatory screws. There was no bag to catch the tails of the control lines. There was only one instead of three mandatory buckets. And, finally, the zippers on two of our vest-type life jackets were broken. In my initial review of the boat, I noticed all of these problems, but did nothing to fix them.

This is a good example of how easy it is for the safety problem to become self-perpetuating with older boats. As boats and equipment get older, they generally don't get the needed upkeep and replacement. The boats then start doing poorly in the racing, which results in the owners having even less interest in spending hours and dollars on their boats. However, the boats still go out to race, and these boats are the first to get into trouble.

As for on-the-water mistakes, both crews had more than enough time to completely remove their harnesses and hobbles from their bodies had they realized the potential danger of being snagged. I learned later that one of my crew had gotten hooked on the forestay twice, but was able to free himself, and I now realize that the forestay, with the jib hanked on every eight inches, was the worst thing to be hanging onto. By hanging onto a shroud instead of the forestay, getting hooked wouldn't have been as immediate a danger, since one could slide freely and thus have more time to clear oneself.

Also, both crews could have bailed with their buckets instead of relying totally on the bailers. We could have postponed our set until most of the water had been drained. Our halyards could have been coiled and stowed better. And, finally, we could have insisted on finding good life jackets before going sailing.

THERE ARE OTHER PRECAUTIONS that should be taken to make your sailing safer. You should check to be sure your boat will float when filled with water, while at the same time realizing that such a test does not duplicate the conditions in which sinkings occur – strong winds, large waves, sails up, etc. Be sure all hiking straps, lines and trapeze wires are in perfect shape so that there is less chance of someone going overboard and being left behind. Always have a knife or two handy somewhere on the boat where you can reach it in a hurry. Be sure your life jacket is comfortable and doesn't restrict movement. It should not be so bulky that it easily catches on things, but it shouldn't be so small or compact that it won't sufficiently float you and any sailing clothing you might be wearing.

Be aware of the danger of getting tangled and being pulled underwater. Above all, don't panic. Struggling against being pulled under often prevents one from getting unsnagged. Once my sister was trapped under a 420 when the boat turtled before she could unhook. Knowing that a turtled dinghy will float above the water, creating some air space, she remained calm, came up inside the boat and unhooked herself. If she had panicked and fought against the hook, she could have been in serious trouble. Another good rule to remember when hitting the water after a capsize is to keep as much air as you can in your lungs and then surface with your hand over your head. If you find yourself under the sail, the quickest way out is to find a seam and follow it to the edge.

Also, every sailor should learn CPR (cardiopulmonary resuscitation) and other lifesaving techniques. Fleets can arrange with local Red Cross chapters for a demonstration and explanation. The question to ask yourself is whether you would know what to do if a person sailing with you started to drown. What if a friend was knocked overboard, swallowed a large amount of water, and was semiconscious? We hope such incidents will never occur, but it is still our responsibility to ourselves and to those sailing with us to have a plan of action ready in case trouble does arise.

There is another important responsibility: reporting any accidents or dangerous situations. Far too many incidents never get reported because people don't want to hurt the reputation of a class or embarrass a sailing area, organization, or other sailors. At the same time, many people don't want to admit that such a thing happened to them, either because they are ashamed of it or because it is a trauma they would just as soon forget. But unless the particulars of such incidents are widely circulated among other sailors, people have little opportunity to learn about the dangers they might face, except through firsthand experience, which is often obtained at a high price and usually just a little too late.

Class newsletters and other yachting publications are ideal means of exposing and helping to eliminate safety problem that most sailors might not even be aware of. After Manton Scott was tragically killed when the mast of the 470 he was helping put away struck some overhead wires in a parking lot, regatta organizers, class magazines, builders, and sailors themselves have constantly reminded others of the dangers of overhead wire around boats, and no doubt many lives have been saved through this increased awareness.

There will always be an element of danger in sailing, no matter how good the sailor or how advanced the boat and equipment. Risk is inherent in a sport whose medium is wind and water. But we can all take large steps toward improving the safety of our racing. We can recognize potential dangers, prepare ourselves for them, and take increased precaution against them. Unfortunately, it's human nature that we are usually shaken into awareness and action only by an immediate tragedy. And it is equally human and unfortunate that our new resolve often fades with time. Having experienced what I did, I pray that none of you will ever have to learn these lessons through tragedy.

Index

About the Author

DAVE PERRY grew up sailing on Long Island Sound. Learning to sail in Sunfish, Blue Jays and Lightnings from his parents and in the junior program at the Pequot Yacht Club in Southport, Connecticut, he won the Clinton M. Bell Trophy for the best junior record on L.I.S. in 1971. While at Yale (1973-77) he was captain of the National Championship Team in 1975, and was voted All-American in 1975 and 1977. Other racing accomplishments include: 1st, 1978 Tasar North Americans; 5th, 1979 Laser Worlds; 1st, 1979 Soling Olympic Pre-Trials (crew); 10th overall, 1981 SORC (crew); 3rd, 1982 Soling Worlds; 1st, 1982 Prince of Wales Match Racing Championship; 1st, 1983 Star South American Championship (crew); 1st, 1983 and 1984 Congressional Cup; 2nd, 1984 Soling Olympic Trials; 6th, 1985 Transpac Race (crew); 1st, 1988 and 1992 Knickerbocker Match Race Cup; and 1st, 1994, 1999 and 2003 Ideal 18 North American Championship.

Dave has been actively working for the sport since 1977. He has led hundreds of US SAILING instructional seminars in over 50 one-design classes; directed U.S. Olympic Yachting Committee Talent Development Clinics; coached the 1981 World Champion U.S. Youth Team; and given seminars in Japan, Australia, Sweden, Argentina, Brazil and Canada. He has been the Youth Representative on the US SAILING Board of Directors and the Chairman of the U.S. Youth Championship Committee, and has served on the following other US SAILING committees: Olympic, Training, Class Racing and O'Day Championship. He is currently a member of the US SAILING Appeals Committee and a US SAILING Senior Certified Judge. In 1992 he was voted into the *Sailing World* Hall of Fame; in 1994 he received an honorary Doctorate of Education from Piedmont College; in 1995 he became the first recipient of US SAILING's Captain Joe Prosser Award for exceptional contribution to sailing education; and in March 2001 Dave received the W. Van Alan Clarke, Jr. Trophy, US SAILING's national award for sportsmanship.

Dave has authored two other books: *Understanding the Racing Rules of Sailing* and *Dave Perry's 100 Best Racing Rules Quizzes*. He is currently the Director of Athletics at Greens Farms Academy, a K-12 coed independent day school in Westport, Connecticut.